1995

Symphony

SYMPHONY

PERCY M. YOUNG

M.A., MUS.D.

WITH ELEVEN DRAWINGS BY

MILEIN COSMAN

CRESCENDO PUBLISHERS

BOSTON

'*The study of the history of music, seconded by hearing the actual performance of the masterpieces of different epochs, will prove the most rapid and effective cure for conceit and vanity.*'

Robert Schumann

Printed in Great Britain
in 10/12 Monotype Garamond by
The Bowering Press of Plymouth for
Crescendo Publishers, Boston
by arrangement with J. M. Dent & Sons Ltd
Aldine House · Bedford Street · London

First published 1957
First published in United States of America 1968

Contents

Most of the illustrations in this book were
specially drawn by Miss Cosman, but those
appearing on pages 65, 117 and the title-page
are reproduced by kind permission of
The Radio Times

INTRODUCTION

FOR AT LEAST two thousand years people have been trying to discover the meaning of music: what it is, why it is, and what it does. But the mystery is too deep for final solution. However, we continue to be fascinated by it, intrigued, and even uplifted by our attempts at comprehension. I am all on the side of those who find music 'difficult to understand'—all music, that is, and not only some specific examples; for one way to genuine pleasure is certainly to attempt to solve aesthetic and spiritual problems as they occur in our own experience.

It may well remove an aura of doubt to realize that of the basic significance of music one person is not demonstrably more aware than another. There is, of course, a degree of misconception on this point. He, or she, who gives an appearance of superior knowledge by readiness in furnishing factual information immediately comes to mind. But to be aware of the correct numbering of, say, Dvořák's symphonies is in itself neither particularly meritorious nor valuable.

This brings us to the point of this book—indeed of the series of which it is a part. There are facts, even 'analyses', such as will no doubt gladden the conscience of the grammar school pupil who needs to pass an examination in music; but there is also some attempt to show why composers wrote works as they did, and why certain music may produce particular reactions of intellect or emotion. The operative word is 'may'. Here one works from one's own experience (basically a Doctor of Music is subject to likes and dislikes as much as the next man—even though he may have some skill in sometimes disguising the fact), and one must therefore show a particular set of inclinations.

This being the case one asks for the kind of companionship that makes a delight of a rural excursion. The issue, however, is larger than this, for it is infinitely more important that the reader should be *en rapport* with the composers, and the works, which line the route of this progress.

Clearly there is a lot to look at, or to listen to; but not all at once. There is a great deal to be said for possessing a few 'favourite' works, or relying on the inspiration of a handful of congenial composers. Even they, however, take on a new complexion when seen in relation to their context, or in contrast with the unfamiliar.

Thus the scheme of this book unfolds. It is for the music-lover, modest, perhaps, in his attainments. It has something about history, something about structural principles, something about the absorbing psychological background to musical expression and appreciation, and something about those factors common to all the arts. It is hoped it will be a concert-goer's or discophile's ready reckoner. If occasionally it strays towards the academic it is because I believe musical literacy to be generally desirable. So it is sometimes proposed that miniature scores of works should be consulted—an excellent way, incidentally, to feel sympathy with the composer who first set his ideas in the notation thus shown. Obviously, however, score-reading must be considered as an optional activity.

In a sense the whole of music is contained in symphony. A glance at Chapter I will show the etymological origins of the word, which make this a reasonable premise. Through three centuries the word has been thus comprehensively understood by composers. That is why one can find what one wants, or needs, in the great symphonies, why the structural principles are necessarily variable, and, consequently, why modern symphonies are different from those of the so-called classical era.

One rather important department of symphony has received scant treatment—the 'programme' symphony. Programme music, it is felt, deserves separate treatment—for it is against the normal symphonic concept that music should paint pictures or rehearse narratives. Which is not to say that programme music may not be very good music, but rather that it is not essentially within the terms of reference of this handbook. Similarly, if choral symphonies appear here to be unjustly done by it is because they fit more happily into a volume on choral music.

P.M.Y.

I. What is a Symphony?

⟨ LOFTY IDEALS · There still hangs over the musical landscape something of the cloud of portentousness that blew up during the nineteenth century. So that those who do not go to 'symphony concerts' regard those who do as possessing some superior capacity of musical understanding; and two out of three orchestras protest high aspirations by dropping the qualifying name into their titles. The 'symphony' orchestra, in fact, spends most of its time in not playing symphonies, and the 'symphony' concert is a compendium of all sorts of music—overtures, variations, suites, excerpts from opera, concertos—and so on. But it is the symphony that is called on to invoke respectability.

I do not suppose that Ernst Pauer is read so widely as formerly. But what he had to say about symphony in the 1870's may be recalled as a warning against too much zeal:

'In the Symphony a certain number of instruments are united, to produce a poetical representation of emotions of the soul. . . . As poetry finds its fullest development in the *drama*, so does

11

instrumental music in the *symphony*; and indeed it may safely be said that the symphony is the highest of all the musical forms, because it demands from the composer an extraordinary amount of power and originality, and an absolutely independent inspiration. The thematic subject must contain in itself the whole idea of the work; from it must be developed all the following logical consequences. But even the invention of an excellent principal subject, and one suitable for all purposes, would be an insufficient guarantee for a good symphony. Many more details have to be considered. A consummate mastery in handling counterpoint, instrumentation, invention of figures, appropriate interpolation of episodes, grouping of phrases, gradation of final effects, and a complete command over all these means, these various important details, is necessary before this greatest of instrumental forms can be satisfactorily constructed. When the architect has drawn the plan of a gorgeous palace, he has many artisans to help him to carry out his idea; not so the composer of a symphony—he must be the architect, the builder, and decorator. No musical form, be it opera, oratorio, or any other, could give us that noble and lofty idea of the wealth and intrinsic power or of the irresistible strength of music that we find in the Symphony.'

❡ RESTRICTED REPERTOIRE · There are, of course, symphonies and symphonies. Some, no doubt, approximate towards the Pauer ideal. A good many, however, do not; yet they have their legitimate place in the scheme of things.

The normal symphonic repertoire is relatively small. Thus a handful of symphonies by Haydn and Mozart represent the eighteenth century, the Stamitz family, the younger Bachs, Dittersdorf, Abel, Gossec—charming composers without exception—being excluded. Of the nineteenth century Beethoven and Brahms are taken as the pre-eminent symphonists. Schubert's 'great' C major symphony gets its place, as also the 'Unfinished'. Of Mendelssohn we are aware of the 'Italian', of Schumann the 'Spring'. of Dvořák the fourth and fifth symphonies. Tchaikovsky provides perhaps three symphonies for the repertoire—but these are rather on probation as lacking in the 'profounder' qualities. Bruckner and Mahler are, at the moment, fashionable but not necessarily very familiar. The twentieth century, being now more than half over, has not yet really caught up with us in the concert hall. Sibelius is firm. But after that? Elgar, Vaughan Williams (whose longevity and fecundity stimulate some sentimental regard), Walton in England; Nielsen in Denmark; Barber, Harris and Copland in the U.S.A.; Malipiero in Italy; Prokofiev and Shostakovich in Russia. The names are known also beyond their own frontiers. But the music less so.

All incipient composers intend to write symphonies before they die. In the course of time they invariably do and in the end composer and symphony die together, both interred in a respectable obituary notice. A discouraging prospect, but apparently no great deterrent, for hopes of musical immortality still reside in 'the noble and lofty idea . . . that we find in the Symphony'. Pauer is not yet quite out-of-date.

⁋ VARIED TYPES · Definitions are notoriously difficult. At first we do not dissent from the *Concise Oxford Dictionary*. A symphony is an 'elaborate orchestral composition of several contrasted but closely related movements'. *Grove's Dictionary* initially takes us a little further (in the long run, of course, a lot further): 'The current meaning, broadly expressed, is a large-scale orchestral work of serious aim, normally in four portions (with or without some interrelationship and theme or mood) termed (from the directions for *tempo*) "movements", at least one of the movements being—again normally—in what is called "sonata" form.'

But we recall that Handel, Bach, and Purcell wrote single movements which they happily termed symphonies; that numerous eighteenth-century symphonies had only three movements; that Beethoven (if we exclude the seventeenth-century Schütz whose motet-type works were called *symphoniae sacrae*) is at the head of a fairly long list of symphonists who used voices as well as instruments; that Roy Harris, indeed, has written a symphony for voices alone; that Haydn wasn't above flippancy; that Sibelius' seventh symphony is in one movement; that whereas Mahler's third symphony lasts for two hours and his eighth, on account of the forces required, was known as 'The Symphony of the Thousand', the five little symphonies of Milhaud, each for a handful of instruments, can all be played within the space of half an hour.

The truth is that normality has no place in art. Because we think it has we become cautious, conservative, censorious; and we stifle imagination. Moreover, the living quality of art is killed and, in self defence, the creative artist tends towards isolation. Thus we arrive at the point where music is written for other musicians, where the guiding principle is far removed from that which inspired composers in previous eras.

❡ URGE AND OPPORTUNITY · The economics of concert-giving are simple. One performance will fill a hall, another will empty it. The first must prevail. Against which may be set, however, a wide range of recorded works and broadcast performances to advance the claims of the unfamiliar. But how may the unfamiliar become ultimately familiar? Piety looks forward to posterity. At the present rate of progress posterity will have its work cut out to deal with the twentieth century. As concert-goers we are mostly content with the achievements of the not-too-distant past. The present hardly exists. And the reason lies partly in an undue reverence for the symphonic grand manner of former days.

Gloomily surveying all the music that is not, and is not likely to be, performed the reader may well be tempted to ask why the urge to compose loses none of its insistence. In answering this we begin to come nearer to the nature of symphonic music.

The justification of living is in making. Sometimes the act has realizable purpose. What we use is immaterial, but in the case of music one makes patterns out of sounds.

First there is the desire to make. Then the consequent desire to make better. Thus one imitates another, fraternities or 'schools' develop, technique increases—even to the extent of becoming an end in itself. At this point art, or for that matter science, tends towards decadence; for the primal reason for making is obscured: the whole is less significant than the parts; the matter than the manner.

❡ MEANING · It is clear that by making an object, whether substantial or insubstantial, one is also communicating. In the first place it is an urge, an ambition, an ideal, but without precise meaning. As, through generations, capacity increases and traditions are evolved a more formal meaning becomes possible. Mediaeval architecture, for instance, is explicit. And, within limits, music too can become explicit. So that one does not greatly differ from Wagner in his summary of Beethoven's Seventh Symphony as 'the apotheosis of the dance'—with all that therein is implied.

The obverse of building is unbuilding:

> *Like a child from the womb,*
> *Like a ghost from the tomb,*
> *I arise and unbuild it again.*

As Shelley so are most creative artists; for to build anew must sometimes involve the clearance of a site. After polyphony comes monody, after tonality atonality, and in the negative lies the positive. How am I, you say, to understand 'modern music'? Perhaps by setting it in opposition to what it replaces. 'Meaning' in music derives from the placing of elements—melodic, rhythmic, harmonic, or instrumental—in contexts which have the authority of convention. It is in this way that the *Eroica* or *Pastoral* symphonies of Beethoven realize their titles. Elements which were, and still are, acceptable as suggesting the heroic ideal on the one hand, or the drama of nature on the other, make possible a comprehension of one art through others.

It may, however, be seen that this 'meaning' is subsidiary to another, and greater. The point about music is not that it is representational, but that it is not. The pictorial or literary symphony may be attractive, amusing, dramatic, or what you will. But the more it is literary, the more it is picturesque, the further it departs from the first principle of musical composition. This is, simply, to make music. Which is not to say, however, that 'literary' music may not achieve its own justification—as will be seen later.

It is the very abstractness of symphonic music, of chamber music, of the 'sonata', that gives rise to the eloquence of Pauer, the solemnity of Grove. And, it is to be remembered, abstractness is the distinctive quality of music.

There is a fascination in watching the historic progress. The one-storey symphony of the seventeenth century; the three-storeys of the early classical era; the four-storeys of the familiar late eighteenth–nineteenth century schools; the sky-scrapers of latter day Romanticism; the more functional and economic use of material in our own time. There are more or less useful analogies in other spheres of activity, and by reference to such analogies we see from one direction why music is as it is.

¶ INSTRUMENTAL MUSIC IN FAVOUR · As in one sense music is the oldest of the arts so in another it is the youngest. That is to say the common knowledge of music hardly extends further back than two centuries or so. The earliest substantial works were for voices, and for performance in church. Settings of psalms, of the 'ordinary' of the Mass, and of other sacred words are among the glories of the middle ages. While such music flourished instrumental music was but a poor-ish relation. We reach the period of the renaissance with instruments subordinate to song and dance. But fetters are made to be broken. Under the new dispensation of a society in which the older values were dispersing, in which, —in accordance with the new idealism—art became a greater social amenity, and aesthetic satisfaction an end in itself, instrumental music established its charms.

In Italy—and indeed in the rest of Europe—consorts of instruments played dances and arrangements of choral music independently. The skill of players and the varied tone colours were enchanting, as every sixteenth- or seventeenth-century writer would testify.

> *When threads can make*
> *A heart-string quake.*
> *Philosophy*
> *Can scarce deny*
> *The soul consists of harmony.*

William Strode, poet and dramatist, shall suffice to indicate the high favour in which music was held in that transitional period, in which the old gradually gave way to the new.

For a time, however, musicians exchanged one service for

another. Formerly music had been ancillary to church ritual. During the seventeenth century it partnered drama. The seventeenth century saw the birth of opera. As we follow the growth of opera we see two significant factors. Through the cultivation of the art of solo singing melody takes wings in *aria*, and by the end of the century the formal method of first section—second contrasted section—repeat of first section is in general use. Secondly, the orchestra is prominent in atmospheric interludes and in the preliminary overture.

¶ SINFONIA · But, in Italian operas of the time of Monteverdi, the overture was not so called. Sometimes the introductory piece was styled *toccata*, but more often *sinfonia*; and so in the opera house, the symphony had its origin. At first the *sinfonia* was brief and to the point—a curtain-raiser; but by the end of the seventeenth century the Italian *sinfonia* had grown into a three-movement work demanding some interest on its own account. The operatic *sinfonia* had in general little close connection with the succeeding drama. Which, perhaps, is not surprising since in effect an opera of that period was a concert in fancy dress. Music, in fact, was asserting its claim to the first place in public interest.

Among a large number of composers the two most prominent during the latter part of the seventeenth century were Lully, Italian-born but a naturalized Frenchman who directed music at the court of Louis XIV, and Alessandro Scarlatti. Both composers were celebrated masters of opera, and each was a pioneer in orchestral method. The type of overture written by Lully was the formal predecessor of the normal three-movement Handelian overture as in opera and oratorio. The pattern was a slow introduction, a fugal *allegro* (each movement descended from choral method), and a finale that was usually a minuet.

In the later *sinfonias* of Scarlatti, on the other hand, there is little to suggest the contrapuntal forms of older music. Lightness, grace, sentiment: these were the objectives. And with stringed instruments they were attainable. Wind instruments had their place in the ensemble, but a modest one.

If we look at a characteristic *sinfonia* by Scarlatti—that to the opera *Griselda*—we discover ourselves on territory not altogether

B

unfamiliar. It is in three movements, but in each of the three are
patent some, at least, of the patterns of later symphonic behaviour.
In the first movement, for instance, a certain solid brilliance. This
is set by rhythm and by the key of D major—that in which trumpets used to find themselves most at home. By way of contrast
the succeeding movement—a 'song without words'—is in minor
tonality, and *adagio* replaces *allegro*. Finally a gay, dance-like
piece in rollicking 6/8 time, and, of course, in D major.

Unity is imposed on music in various ways, but from the time
of Scarlatti until yesterday, or the day before, the most significant,
material, unity was tonal. It is, therefore, not unimportant to
recognize the relationship between key centres which then obtained.

In the *sinfonia* of Scarlatti the music may be perceived (by the
eye) to leave D major (the *tonic*) from time to time. The most
important stops *en route* are in A major (the *dominant*). The slow
movement, however, mostly lies in F sharp minor which, having
the same number of sharps in the key signature as A major is
known as the relative minor to the dominant key. One more key
is encountered—that of E minor. E minor has one sharp (F) in
its signature; so has G major. In relation to D, the basic key of
this particular *sinfonia*, G is known as the *sub-dominant* (not un-
reasonably since, in the keyboard, G is immediately below the
dominant which, as we have discovered, is A). So E minor is the
relative minor to G major.

We go through the classical period, then, aware of tonic, sub-
dominant, dominant, and their relative minors—or, if the tonic
is minor, majors: a sort of closed shop, which, fortunately, did
not remain closed for long.

❡ THE EIGHTEENTH CENTURY · The Scarlatti model caught on
and a succession of composers improved on the symphonic
prototype. Among Italian composers one of the principal was
Giovanni Battista Sammartini, of Milan. A prolific writer with a
total list of some two thousand works Sammartini enlarged the
symphony. If we look at the first movement of one of his symphonies we find this design: an initial theme in the tonic followed
by a gradual movement (or *modulation*) to the dominant, wherein

stands *new melodic material*. The themes in themselves are, per-haps, commonplace but there is clearly a considerable pleasure in their setting out for instruments, as in their dovetailing. The second melodic group comes to a clear terminus in the dominant. But this is no more than the exordium. We are immediately off again. A new section starts from where we left off—in the key of the dominant. But the melody is at first as at the outset of the movement: a familiar character or idea in a new light. Now the progress is back towards the controlling tonic key. At the moment of arrival the first theme, now making its third appearance, comes once again, and we are carried safe home to a firm conclusion in the tonic.

Altogether an agreeable pattern. Clear, easy to follow, and saleable. Sammartini built up a considerable reputation as teacher, and composers came from far and near to learn his method. Three-movement symphonies (sometimes they were called over-tures) sprouted everywhere. If we used the conventional terms of contemporary popular evaluation we should call these Italian pieces 'light music'.

Heredity and environment, however, have a good deal to do with musical expression. Each country possesses its own musical ethos, created by centuries of adaptation to local demands. German music of whatever age has an unmistakable earnestness; Czech music a startling degree of fire; Austrian music a capacity for synthesis, so that it displays influences from Germany, Bohemia, and Italy, but is nonetheless wholly individual. While Sammartini and his disciples worked at symphony and sonata (of which the form is virtually the same as the symphony) in the south, C. P. E. Bach developed the new style in the north. And to Mannheim came a number of Bohemian composers, of whom members of the Stamitz family were the best known, to add their contribution. By the 1760's more dramatic effects were audible within symphony, derived from a keener appreciation of har-monic and orchestral resources and from greater melodic variety.

By now the first movement may be represented thus: theme 1 (tonic) leading to theme 2 (which sometimes is a group of themes) (dominant): repetition of previous thematic material (dominant) leading to repetition of theme (or group) 2 (tonic).

There are numerous works on the fringes of the normal repertoire which can give great delight both to performers and listeners: among these the symphonies of Abel, Dittersdorf, the younger Stamitz, Gyrowetz, Filtz, Wagenseil, and the Earl of Kelly—a Scottish nobleman who studied at Mannheim—in which it may be felt how the age expressed its ideal of sweet reasonableness in terms of music. In general, however, one lesser master appears much as another. Therefore we turn to Haydn, who wrote symphonies for nearly half a century, and to Mozart, assuming their works to comprehend those of their less prominent contemporaries.

The younger Bachs, the Stamitz dynasty, the Dittersdorfs, and so on, were clearly highly thought of in their own day, to which their works were apt. And so it appears to us. For their limitations, indeed, we may well be grateful. The general precision of statement and apparent disregard of tempestuous emotions furnish an agreeable contrast to the more expansive self-revelations of the later Romantic mood.

❡ DEVELOPING FORM · The early symphonies both of Haydn and Mozart are reflective of the culture of the aristocracy, and are best enjoyed as chamber music in a not too large auditorium. In the later symphonies of these composers, however, there is a more public quality. The music is larger in every way. The movements have expanded; there are more instruments involved; there is more dynamic range.

Formally, these features are to be noted. Before the first movement proper, in Haydn but not often in Mozart, there may be set a slow introduction. The thematic material of the movement is more highly organized than previously; there are two themes, or groups of themes, showing the same key relationships as before but united by other material that is more than mere passage work. This *exposition*, its end marked by a firm cadence, was normally repeated—by which means the listener was made fully aware of the basic themes of the dialectic. After the exposition the music ranges fairly widely through nearly (and sometimes not so nearly) related keys, but within this part of the score the composer discussed ideas previously set out in the exposition. One need not quarrel with the formal academic designation of this section as the *development*. After the development the *recapitulation*, wherein the exposition is repeated, with certain modifications. Of these the most obvious is the appearance of the second group of themes in the tonic and not, as before, in the dominant. At the end of the recapitulation frequently lies a *coda*, an end flourish, an index, or what you will. No two movements are exactly alike but this general scheme served as the common ground plan of music for at least a century and a quarter.

In slow movements, too, the influence of this 'sonata' form prevailed, except that the centre block—the development—was omitted. At the same time we should note that Haydn frequently favoured the older and always intriguing pattern of air and variations—as in the 'surprise' symphony.

For some time the minuet—and trio, which had its place in the older suite—had been within the suburbs of symphony. Sometimes in the earlier masters it made a finale. From about 1765, however, when Haydn wrote his symphony 31, the minuet formed a third movement, to be followed by a rondo finale. Although there are exceptions to practically everything that has been stated (for art observes principles rather than rules) this four-movement structure became the norm, and within each movement there was a high degree of organization.

The classical symphony, as we might expect, presupposes certain experience on the part of the listener. Cutting up symphonies into little bits is not my idea of fun, but to have a prior appreciation of the structural principles is as essential as anything can be said to be essential.

We see, however, that the structure of symphony leads in itself to certain emotional conclusions. The relative complexity of first movement design appeals in some considerable degree to the intellect. The inevitably slower tempo of the succeeding movement, its tendency to emulate song, its reduction of tonal temperature (for the slow movement was normally in the key of the sub-dominant), all strike more directly at the emotions. After

which the minuet and trio, back in the tonic key, afford relaxa-
tion; while the last movement, quick and more often than not
rather more thought-free than the first movement, sends us home
content with the simple belief that everything will come right
in the end.

❡ IMPACT OF NEW IDEAS · At this point the clever reader might
sit down and write a symphony according to prescription. In so
doing he would be following in the footsteps of more than one
great composer—Wagner, for instance, or Elgar. But the result
would be somewhat unsatisfying. For at no time was music
rigidly fixed within hard-and-fast formulas. Haydn and Mozart
moved on through the last part of the eighteenth century aware
that circumstances of life and thought were for ever mutable.
Rousseau's *La Nouvelle Héloïse* was published in 1761, and his
Contrat social a year later; Herder, Goethe, and Schiller were
near-contemporaries of Haydn and Mozart; Klinger added to our
stock of catch phrases the term *Sturm und Drang*. Music as a quasi-
philosophical means of expression became increasingly important.
So we are taught to discern, especially in the last three symphonies
of Mozart, a more material significance in music. One has only to
look at *The Magic Flute* on the one hand and the *Creation* or *The
Seasons* on the other to see that Mozart and Haydn did indeed
subscribe to the belief that music could be more than music. It
will, however, be concluded that Mozart's symphonies—the
'Jupiter' designation of No. 41 has no authority—give no direct
extra-musical references and that the familiar sub-titles of Haydn's
are of no great significance.

With Beethoven it is different. The third of his symphonies is
an 'heroic symphony composed to celebrate the memory of a
great man'. And the slow movement—of vast, heroic dimensions
—is a funeral march. By now we are quite certain that the music
is 'about' something. 'Music', Beethoven wrote in 1810, 'is a
higher revelation than the whole of wisdom and the whole of
philosophy.' At another time he postulated that 'music ought to
create and fan the fire of the spirit of man'. And yet again: 'There
is no rule which one cannot break for the sake of beauty.'

With the first two sentiments I suspect the common run of

listeners are in sympathy. Philosophers and contemporary composers, on the other hand, are sceptical of such extravagant
utterance, which has no justified association with formal logic.
In respect of 'rule-breaking', however, the listener will concede
Beethoven's right, but dispute that of anyone else.

Beethoven's bouts of iconoclasm were judiciously directed, and
no man more heartily sustained the validity of great traditions.
Handel and Bach, Haydn and Mozart: these were great beyond
any dispute. The principles of design of sonata and symphony
were for Beethoven not limiting, but limitless. In the first two
symphonies one is not always aware that the eighteenth century
is past. True, the opening of the first is explosive by Haydnesque
standards, and the third movement of the second has such
piquancy as is proposed by the new definition—*scherzo*. And,
especially in the slow movements, there is an amplitude in melody,
harmony, and orchestration that is felt to indicate a new approach
in music to 'the spirit of man'.

Beethoven, whose works will be considered in greater detail
in Chapter V, widened the scope of all music and, therefore, of
symphonic music. Formal considerations were secondary to
philosophic purpose—though formlessness, being a negation of
coherent expression, was by no means the desired end. If more
movements than four were required (as in the *Pastoral* symphony)
then more there should be. Colour—both harmonic and instrumental—was available to the artist and should be freely employed.
Striking effects of tonal and dynamic contrast, of the hitherto
underprivileged percussion department, were the means where-
by souls might be won. If the phrase sounds overpitched remember that Beethoven had a missionary zeal. Not only should music
become universal, but through its influence mankind should
achieve the millennium of universal brotherhood: 'Menschen
werden Brüder'—the motto of the ninth symphony.

❡ SELF-EXPRESSION · All this was one side of Romanticism—
the expression of general ideas. On the other was self-expression
as an end in itself. Of this the great exemplar was Berlioz, whose
Fantastic Symphony, first performed three years after the death of
Beethoven, is one of music's most intriguing autobiographical

statements. At this point the germ of decadence is to be detected. In classical music—which also means that of Beethoven—one may feel the quality of pity: in romantic music, at some levels, it is more evidently self-pity. To be able to discuss music in such terms is something of a convenience, but we are often left at the mercy of intuition; and our assessment of Schumann, Liszt, Franck, Bruckner, Mahler, Tchaikovsky, for instance, depends largely on personal feelings. There seems no absolute criterion. Whether these composers 'developed' symphonic form by inter-linked movements, the exploitation of 'motto' themes, the increasing expansion of the orchestra, is interesting, but largely irrelevant. What appears to matter (it certainly mattered to the composers) is 'meaning'.

But Schubert, Mendelssohn, Brahms, Dvořák, Sibelius are of another order. However much we try to read into their symphonies they finally elude words. (Mendelssohn toys with picturesqueness but not, in my opinion, in such manner as to destroy his essentially classical quality.) For them music was its own justification.

Symphonic composition is a matter of musical architecture. The classical writer plans his edifice and leaves his clients to find out for themselves how to live within it. The Romantic, on the other hand, either lives in his creation himself or instructs his friends on their *modus vivendi*. From the attitude of the composer, then, form develops, or deteriorates.

❡ A CHANGE OF NATURE · The end of the romantic symphony was the symphonic poem, in which, often, the poetry was apparently more momentous than the music. Perhaps the composer did not intend that this should be the case, but one has only to read programme notes to see where significance has been assumed to lie. So one may turn with relish to the verbal expositions of, say, Strauss's three early symphonic poems: *Don Juan*, *Macbeth*, and *Tod und Verklärung*, which are among the grandest and most grandiose of their kind.

Progress is normally regarded as going forward. In music, however, at least there is often a sense of *reculer pour mieux sauter*. Pictorialism, for instance, was one feature, if only a minor one, of Elizabethan music where virginals music sometimes quaintly attempts the martial, and frequently engages in landscape. And nationalism, which 'ism' attached itself to music during the Romantic era, first preened itself in the feathers of the folk-singers of time past. Some of the flavour of Haydn undoubtedly derives from Croatian song, but it was not really until the Russians began to react against the air of superiority worn by the German academicians that symphonies of which the principal themes were either folk tunes or based on folk tune idiom came into fashion. Familiar Russian examples of such music are Tchaikovsky's second ('Little Russian') and Borodin's second symphony, where the quotations are direct. In Dvořák the spirit of folk music is assimilated and distilled with genius; and, perhaps, the same might be said of Vaughan Williams's *Pastoral Symphony*. Those with a geographic bent may travel symphonically or rhapsodic-ally round the world in an armchair. And if dissatisfied with this world one may attempt the next, in the company of Olivier Messiaen. This composer, incidentally, may be said to hold one symphonic record: his *Turangalila*, commissioned by the Kous-sevitzky Foundation in 1949, is in ten movements.

So far two basic principles have obtained. Whatever the *purpose* of symphonic music the formal patterns crystallized in the latter part of the eighteenth century were, even if obscured, never lost sight of; and the inter-relationship of keys, even if the family more and more admitted distant cousins, stood firm so that Bernard Shaw could rightly observe that 'as long as there was a keynote there was no fundamental difference between Bach and Richard Strauss'. True 'harmonic practice was so free that the scale became a 12-note scale with nothing of the old tonality left but a keynote'. The keynote, however, was the lode-star. Even now (as in such 'tonal' works as Vaughan Williams's sixth symphony) it may be demonstrated that atonality is not in itself a guarantee of musical progress.

⁋ NEWER FORMS OF DISCIPLINE · Atonality (more or less con-temporary with bitonality—two keys at once—and polytonality —a lot of keys at once) and polyrhythm, however, at least served the purpose of bringing composers back to a recognition of the existence of music as a thing in itself. And in dispensing with one form of discipline it was necessary to impose others. Hence the systematization of the disciples of Schoenberg, which is as restrictive as the schemes imposed by mediaeval schoolmen. Without attempting to invent a new language of music other composers have brought into the symphonic *ethos* practices of the pre-classical. Brahms indeed saw possibilities in this, as shown in the concluding—*passacaglia*—movement of the fourth symphony. The rehabilitation of counterpoint in modern musical technique has, however, been in large measure due to the practice and preaching of Hindemith.

In many ways the present is akin to the seventeenth century in the proliferation of new and startling ideas. Modern music is incomprehensible if we use nineteenth-century ears for its absorption; but comes within the field of intelligibility if we add up all our musical experience. There is, in fact, no one specific modern style any more than in poetry or in painting. There are, however, two definable classes of works, which stem from two separate points of view. Some music avoids the listener like the plague— a fair amount of this is dodecaphonic (blessed word!): some goes some way to meet him.

❨ NEW WORLD SYMPHONIST · How a contemporary composer may set out to meet the listener half way may be seen in, say, the seven symphonies of the American composer Roy Harris. His expressed opinions, which usefully summarize his own music, bring us back to fundamentals, for so Mozart might have written: 'Music must be just as cogent and logical and structurally perfect as [the composer] can make it. But its form must be determined by its content. It must grow as a plant or an animal grows, along lines dictated by its own inner necessity, not imposed on it from above.'

A composer like Harris whose style incorporates mediaeval, baroque, and classical elements, who is at once romantic and anti-romantic, nationalist and internationalist, is not easy to classify. And that is one main difficulty about 'appreciating' much contemporary work. But classification is not the end, nor yet is it the beginning of appreciation. From which we may go to that which gives life to symphony—the orchestra.

II. The Medium

❰ 'SYMPHONY ORCHESTRA' · It would be inconceivable that an artist in making a painting should first complete a detailed drawing and then—and then only—begin to consider the matter of colour. It should be equally inconceivable that a composer in designing an orchestral work should 'get the notes right' before thinking about their physical presentation. As a matter of fact, and this is one of the attractive properties of contemporary music, most composers don't. Indeed, it may be felt sometimes that brilliant instrumentation disguises thinnish thought. But that is a matter of opinion, and I have no doubt that in the days of Alessandro Scarlatti wiseacres shook their heads at the new instrumental *tours de force* in the early *sinfonias* which were, it appeared, at the expense of the old, proved, thoughtful ways.

STRINGS · The concertgoer of to-day is faced with a company of perhaps ninety or a hundred players, or even more. Of these players the largest number are concerned with stringed instruments. To the conductor's left are first and second violins; in the B.B.C. Symphony Orchestra 20 of the one and 18 of the other. To his right the cellos—12 in number; behind them 8 double basses. Then, the treble and bass members of the string family are united by the middle-range violas, of which there are 14. From the seventeenth century, when violins finally ousted the older viols (from which as its shape shows the double-bass is descended), this has been the mainstay of the orchestral ensemble.

The viola, however, was rather a late starter. When, as in the early days of the *sinfonia*, melody was all-important and brilliance the chief of the virtues of recreational music, inner parts—such as the viola is mostly bound to play—were discouraged. And there was, because of the prevailing fashion, little incentive to anyone to learn the viola. In Handel's day the worst of the fiddlers were put on to the 'tenor' as the viola was called. In some earlier symphonies of Mozart and Haydn it will be noticed that although the violas are included they rarely play independently of the cellos. It was the Romantic period, when it was desired to exploit every emotional potentiality in the tone-colour palette, which raised the status of the viola community.

Until the nineteenth century the function of stringed instruments was largely linear. The first violins played the top line—the 'tune'; the cellos—reinforced by the double-basses who played the same part an octave lower, thus adding 16ft tone—the bass line. The second violins and violas (when they were emancipated to this point) wove inner patterns of greater or lesser interest. Thus all was, or should have been, clarity in the string department.

But, as Handel (a wonderfully imaginative orchestrator) had shown, new effects could be produced by different organization of the string ensemble. In the 'Pastoral' symphony of *Messiah*, for instance, Handel divided his violins into three parts. (That this music is rarely played according to his intention makes no difference to the effectiveness of his idea.) And, of course, Bach achieved thrilling sonorities in the string writing of the third and sixth Brandenburg concertos. In these, however, the delight in tone for its own sake is less than that in the marvellous interplay of contrapuntal designs.

By way of contrast listen to the minor *adagio ma non troppo* within the introduction to the last movement of Beethoven's choral symphony. Here violins are silent, violas are divided into three, and cellos into two parts to evoke solemnity. Once this poetical exploitation of string tone had been demonstrated composers dispensed with the proposition that the duty of strings was to play in four parts. Listen now, therefore, to the function of the strings in the last movement ('Witches' Sabbath') of Berlioz's 'Fantastic' symphony; to the *adagio espressivo* of Schumann's second symphony in C (where the intensity of the feeling is deepened by the full middle harmonies of divided violas); to the frequent use of upper strings, divided, in Vaughan Williams's *Sinfonia Antartica*; or to Elgar's second symphony in E flat, which, throughout, is masterly in manipulation of string tone.

These being, broadly speaking, all romantic works we sense the application of string tone, as colour, and with some specific reference. The tone is evocative. We are reminded of witches, of cultivated melancholy (Schumann's speciality), of icebergs, of regality, and funereal pomp. Very moving; very beautiful; very clever. So we may applaud. But the purpose of music? Has it, or has it not been forgotten? We turn to music which reacts against what basically is sentimental.

Most interesting, and grievously ignored, is the second *Serenade* of Brahms in A major, composed in 1859 (but revised in 1875) for the court orchestra at Detmold. From this work violins are entirely excluded. (In the first movement of his *Requiem* Brahms again similarly reduces the string colour.) Both the *Serenades* are, in fact, very much essays in the classical, Haydn, manner.

The rehabilitation of reason as a mainspring of musical creation has tended to a reduction in orchestral 'colour'. Or, alternatively, to a realization of new colour schemes in more economical formations of instruments. The *Chamber Symphony* (see Schoenberg, Webern, Hindemith) of the twentieth century usually represents the new classicism. Linear music, unemotional music, intellectual music; though not necessarily to the common taste. In such works the orchestration is slender and string players sometimes find that their lease has expired. In his *Kammersymphonie* Anton Heiller wrote for oboe, clarinet, bassoon, violin, viola, and cello. Webern's *Symphonie* (Op. 21) is for clarinet, bass clarinet, two horns, harp, and strings without double-basses. Sometimes, as in Walther Gmeindl's *Kammersymphonie* for twenty-four instruments, the number of strings to be employed is specified: two and two only, of each. In the *Symphony of Psalms* (which according to the conventions is, of course, no symphony) Stravinsky uses no strings, except for cellos and double-basses, which play a purely supporting role.

The supremacy of the strings is not ended (nor perhaps will it be); but the symphonic responsibility of woodwind, brass, and even percussion is greater than was formerly the case.

WOODWIND · As you look at the orchestra in the concert hall you see behind the massed body of strings the long line of woodwind. As you examine an orchestral score you discover this group at the top of the page (the strings are at the bottom). Whether you study the players in a performance or observe the details of notation you will see that whereas the strings remain constant—in that the normal score, even when the strings are divided, shows violins I and II, violas, cellos, double-basses—the woodwind vary from work to work. In the *Sinfonia avanti l'opera* of Scarlatti's *La Griselda* (1721) the woodwind is limited to two oboes. A good deal of their time they occupy in filling in harmony notes which could be dispensed with without any great detriment to the music. Once or twice, however, in the outer movements they put on a brave show of their own. In the first movement they martially demonstrate their willingness to take on the two trumpets; in the last movement they fly about in emulation of the strings. In the slow movement all the wind is silent. It may be presumed, although the score does not show it, that bassoons (if available) doubled the string bass.

Oboes and bassoons, being double-reed instruments, form a complete family. In the pre-symphonic days wind instruments were conspicuous for their family loyalty. Recorders made in all sizes formed a consort, the shawms (from which come the oboe-bassoon group) another. In the reorganization of instrumental ensemble most woodwind instruments lost their place. But in the years between then and now the families have been re-assembled.

Of the symphonic composers who succeeded Scarlatti one of

the most conspicuous was Johann Stamitz. In charge of the most celebrated orchestra of his day, that of the Electoral Court at Mannheim, he was able to spread himself in the matter of orchestration. His scores show two flutes, two oboes, two bassoons; jointly, and with the horns, they filled the score from time to time with a flood of rich tone. It was exciting—even if the woodwind erred, as sometimes they did, in intonation—and novel. Wind music, more conspicuous in out-of-doors serenades and cassations, was becoming domesticated.

Every orchestra, however, was not so well endowed with competence as that of Mannheim and in the symphonies of Abel and J. C. Bach, and the early symphonies of Haydn and Mozart, oboes, horns, and bassoons alone were allowed for. Often they were by no means indispensable. If there were flutes but no oboes the parts could be given to the former. Occasionally the oboes (or flutes) were permitted solo passages; nothing much more than a brief arpeggio, or a scale passage, often played by the two instruments in thirds. A host of agreeable music for amateur instrumentalists lies within this period, and everything arrangeable, if need be, for violins, cellos and basses, and pianoforte. Our first symphonists were nothing if not practical.

In the later symphonies of Haydn the woodwind department was rationalized as two flutes, two oboes, two bassoons: what, in fact, Stamitz had postulated thirty years previously. But, looking in particular at the score of 'The Clock' symphony, the players have by now come into their own. The tone of violins may be edged by the quiet radiance of flute (as happens in the first movement); *crescendo* may be the more effectively outlined by the reinforcement of strings by the woodwind family; or dramatic rhythmic gestures may be shown up; strings may move with more apparent power when sustained wind chords act as a springboard; or—as in the slow movement which gives the familiar title to the symphony—new ranges of tonal beauty may be revealed in the more or less extensive solo or duet episodes. In 'The Clock' symphony one should spare an ear for the flighted fancies of flutes and bassoon in the trio of the third movement. We must keep an eye on this section of symphony, for this is

where, in the classical period, the woodwind often has a day
out.

We may turn to the trio of Mozart's symphony 39, in E flat.
Herein is at once shown a new voice; that of the clarinet. Neither
Haydn nor Mozart made additions to a score simply because they
wanted more noise. Variety of tone colour, yes; but that was a
different matter. Mozart, whose affection for the clarinet went
back to the time of his visit to Mannheim in 1777, came to see its
potentialities more fully through his acquaintance with the
Viennese player Anton Stadler (for whom were written the
clarinet quintet and the concerto). So the clarinet was established
in the concert-room orchestra, its previous existence being either
in open-air or theatre music.

So in Beethoven's scores are two each of flutes, oboes, clarinets,
bassoons.

No sooner, however, had the constitution of the 'symphony'
orchestra been settled than someone suggested further expansion.
Occasionally Haydn and Mozart (in oratorio and opera) wanted
to make music realistic. And this is where wind instruments,
whose technical capacity was increasing all the time through the
genius and persistence of instrument makers, came into their
own. Notice the piccolo's attempt at sheet lightning in the
'Pastoral' symphony, as well as the bird noises of the slow
movement.

And now look at Berlioz's score in the *Symphonie fantastique*.
Above the two flutes in the score is the piccolo, the second
flautist playing the piccolo as required. In the *Scène aux champs* is
a cor anglais, which is played by the second oboist.

'In expressing ideas of sorrow and regret', wrote Cecil Forsyth,
'the instrument seems to have almost more personality than any
other in the orchestra.' Berlioz in the instance quoted puts the
shepherd with his pipe into the landscape and throws in his quota
of sorrow and regret as well. Later the cor anglais became indispensable, when the suggestion of such qualities was required, as
frequently it was. In the matter of colour Berlioz spared no expense. The piccolo could be played by a disengaged flautist, the
cor anglais by the oboist, the little E flat clarinet (which makes

derisory entry into the 'Witches' Sabbath') by the second clari-
nettist. But if four bassoons were necessary, as they were, particularly for the horrifics of the last movement, then two extra
players must be engaged.

Through the nineteenth century interest in woodwind playing
increased. And technique appreciated also. In the spacious days
of the end of the century and the opening years of the present
century it was, if you were lucky with your orchestra, more or
less possible to have what instruments you wanted. Composers
of symphonies were less extravagant than the symphonic poets,
but even Brahms added a double-bassoon to his scores—and with
what profundity it underlines the opening of the first symphony.

Instruments supplementary to the double wood-wind chorus
first made occasional appearances. Brahms, Tchaikovsky, and
Dvořák managed for the most part with the same resources as
Beethoven. But the expanding opera orchestra, the desire to be
more and more expressive, made it inevitable that some of the
part-timers should become full-timers. Not all composers were as
ambitious as Mahler, or the Swedish composer Alfvén, who went
so far as to have quadruple woodwind; but to accommodate the
majority of latter-day composers the woodwind complement
nowadays normally incorporates—as in the *Sinfonia Antartica* of
Vaughan Williams—three flutes (one of which alternates with
piccolo), two oboes and cor anglais, two clarinets and bass
clarinet, two bassoons and double bassoon. The saxophone (alto
or tenor) is an occasional visitor (see Honegger's *Skating-Rink*:
Tanz Symphonie), but its dubious credentials militate against its
regular employment.

In the music of Haydn and Mozart one does not bother over-
much with the 'personality' of instruments. In symphonic music
of the Romantic era (in which many of us still live) it is a feature
of some importance. But the revival of classical and pre-classical
values has lessened the significance of this factor. Instruments are
instruments. Their function is to draw lines, and perhaps, to
draw them more incisively than do the strings. Hence the harder
edge of woodwind as in Stravinsky, Vaughan Williams, Walton,
Rubbra. . . . We may, perhaps, find the later symphonic works of

C

these composers rather less than colourful—unless our standards
are adjusted.

BRASS · The reaction, as in painting, was, however, inevitable.
The 'spirit of the age' has much to account for. Drab, economic,
functional, scientific, are words which may spring easily to mind
after reading the last sentence or two and after hearing the music
to which they refer. And in respect of Wagner or Bruckner or
Elgar it is difficult to avoid—even if the intention is derogatory
—reference to the 'heroic'. In this connotation the brass, raised
still higher on the stage of the concert hall and above the ranks
of the woodwind, are specially favoured.

Our first Queen Elizabeth had strong ears as well as a strong
stomach. During dinnertime she was, sometimes at least, enter-
tained by two dozen trumpeters and drummers. Trumpets were
the special symbol of royalty, and the more of them on view the
better it was for public relations. And if the Queen went hunting
—as at Kenilworth—her progress was marked by the fanfaronade
of hunting horns. Church ceremonial, on the other hand, was
given greater aural dignity by the presence of trombones.

Thus early were these brass instruments endowed with a certain 'personality'. To what extent the character which we attribute
to instruments is because of association and usage, or physical reaction to the particular properties of timbre—which depends on
the respective acoustic arrangement of harmonics deriving from
the material and structure of the instrument—is impossible to
decide. But we are conditioned so that we are inclined to react
in a particular way to particular timbres. And no instruments
are more powerful in their immediate action on sensibility than
the brass.

During the Renaissance and Baroque periods trumpeters
especially were favoured members of the musical fraternity. An
astonishing degree of virtuosity developed so that by the Bach–
Handel era trumpet parts of quite fantastic brilliance were commonplace. But then, suddenly the skill evaporated. Fewer trumpeters were in employment in royal establishments and the
'classical' orchestra found no place for the spectacular roulades
of the previous period. One can see why. When Bach or Handel

used a solo trumpet in an orchestral work it was the trumpet or
nothing. The symphony called for co-operation and a degree of
tact which the brass family appeared not to possess. Moreover,
both trumpets and horns, natural and unvalved instruments,
were severely limited. Except in the upper reaches they could
play no more than the notes of the common chord. As for
changing key; that could only be done by inserting a crook either
to lengthen (and therefore sharpen) or to shorten (and flatten)
the pitch.

However, the horn especially had a wonderful binding tone,
which would agree either with oboes and bassoons, and, later,
the woodwind generally, or with strings. The horns—always in
pairs—won their symphonic place early. But, until the introduction of valves in the early nineteenth century, which gave a complete chromatic range, horn parts laboured under an obvious dis-
ability. As a matter of fact the gaps between the notes of the
natural harmonic series were partially bridged by the formation
of other notes by hand-stopping—i.e. by putting the hand in the
bell of the instrument. And, of course, composers of genius were
able to cut their coat according to their cloth.

Consider, for instance, the significant horn and trumpet parts
of Mozart's Symphony in C (K. 425 'The Linz') or the spectacular
horn parts in the scherzo of the *Eroica*. The brass writing of
Beethoven is worthy of the closest scrutiny, for he employed all
his orchestra with his ear attuned to the potential expressive
capacity of each instrument. To that we may look in greater detail
in another chapter, but here we may note the first symphonic
appearance of trombones in the fifth symphony.

By the middle of the nineteenth century the valve mechanism
of horns and trumpets allowed great flexibility, and, obviously,
the emotional range of these instruments was increased. And the
trombone had established itself. So the layout of the brass department was four horns, two trumpets, three trombones (see
Brahms's first symphony). Note that the horns have, since the
classical period, multiplied. But the nineteenth century was a
period in which chords as such had acquired a particular merit,
and each department of the orchestra became a self-contained

unit capable of playing such striking chordal progressions as may
be discovered in the introductory bars of the slow movement of
Dvořák's 'New World' symphony, or in the last movement of
Brahms's fourth symphony.

While instrument makers were experimenting with the valve
trumpet (in passing we might note the keyed trumpet which had
a short vogue and for which Haydn wrote his trumpet concerto)
there was also evolved the cornet-à-pistons. This instrument, the
maid-of-all-work of the military band, enjoyed great popularity
in France and thus occurs in the scores of Berlioz and Franck.
Elgar makes entertaining use of the cornet in *Cockaigne*, but it has
never been generally regarded as other than rather a shabby
wanton so far as 'serious' music is concerned.

In the scores of Bruckner is met another class of instrument
that has not been greeted with other than lukewarm enthusiasm
outside Austria and Germany: the tuba. Developed in Germany
for military bands, tubas caught the ear and imagination of
Wagner, who promptly introduced them *en famille* into the
orchestra; a new tone colour.

In general one tuba—the bass tuba—keeps its place, as support
to the bass trombone. Accordingly you may now expect to see in
the brass department of the 'symphony' orchestra—four horns;
two (sometimes three) trumpets; three trombones; tuba. You
may also understand how it is that after playing the national
anthem, and perhaps the inevitable overture that commences
most concerts, a good many of the brass contingent disappear
into the band room for a game of cards—until they re-emerge for
some gargantuan piece of more or less modern times.

PERCUSSION · The twin sources of music are song and dance;
from one melody, from the other rhythm disentangle themselves
as the prime factors. Song had a long innings and devotion first
to strings and then to woodwind instruments centred on their
ability to sing; while brass instruments were envisaged as a
superior sort of chorus. My friends tell me—sometimes with and
sometimes without justification—that 'modern' music is un-
melodic. By which they mean that it does not sing. The 'I like a
tune' complex focusses on melodies which can transmute them-

selves into bathroom ballads; nor are they necessarily the worse for that. Now song and dance lived together so agreeably for so long that the primal urge of dance lost something of its first vitality. And music tended away from the common understanding.

At the present time the balance has been rather more than re-dressed. We are a good deal more than rhythm-conscious, even if we are no more rhythmic. Rhythm in fact is an obsession. So much so that in the higher branches of musical composition young men contrive such rhythmic complexity that their music is unperformable, while a self-respecting symphonist can hardly show his face without a complete percussion band in attendance. Vaughan Williams has lately had a playful half-hour with this department in his eighth symphony. In his earlier symphonies timpani, triangle, bass drums, and cymbals appeared. But now we go all the way with—as the composer says—'all the 'phones and 'spiels' in addition. The dance band has nothing on a modern symphony orchestra in the matter of percussion.

Not really a percussion instrument, but with the capacity to edge rhythm, the harp (sometimes two harps) is placed below the percussion in the score, and to the rear of the fiddlers on the platform. Also lying on the outskirts of percussion may be found the pianoforte—brought in almost always as a percussion extra, as in the *Symphony of Psalms*, or as in symphonies by Alfvén, Foerster, Genzmer, Vaughan Williams, and others. It should be remembered that the eighteenth-century orchestra also contained a keyboard instrument; but the harpsichord only held its place as a relic from former days when without it there would have been no middle harmony.

There is, clearly, no end to the percussion possibilities. In non-symphonic music we can go as far as clanking chains (Strauss and Schoenberg), type-writers (Antheil), vacuum cleaners (Arnold), in symphonic music as far as the banjoes, mandolins, and guitars of Křenek's *Kleine Symphonie* (Op. 58). Nothing, how-ever, is so old as the new: Vivaldi employed a pair of mandolins in one of his concertos.

When Virgil Thomson heard one of his own works, scored for an unusual combination, he commented that it made a 'funny noise'.

Experiment, of course, is the life-blood of music, and, just now, experimentation with instrumental timbres is particularly widespread. There is, however, another point. Especially in the U.S.A. the worthy ideal of 'music for the masses' stands prominent in the musician's conscience. Hence, the belief that one may perhaps find the way to higher things up a staircase of percussion instruments.

III. The Symphony Today

('MODERN' AND 'CONTEMPORARY' · Did we live in a more homogeneous society the word 'contemporary' would have no more than its limited significance—see *Concise Oxford English Dictionary*. Alas! 'Contemporary' is now, as applied to the arts, a term of abuse, slightly more opprobrious than 'modern'. 'I do not', says he or she who has made a point of never hearing any, 'like modern music.'

Of course, time does not stand still, and when in a year or two any works quoted in this chapter are referred to again they may well appear positively out-of-date. I am of such vintage that now I may look back affectionately at my first music-master, to whom none other than Brahms was an outrage. We take it, then, that there are those who by nature are antipathetic to anything new in music.

At the same time it might be pointed out that this attitude itself is of fairly recent date. In the eighteenth century, for instance, anything that was not up-to-date in music was deplored. A new symphony in the 1780's needed as many contemporary gadgets to justify itself as a present-day motor-car or washing machine. But the latter, you say, are useful. And so, say I, with an eye on the

television or cinema screen, or with memories of a commission
to compose a score for a civic occasion, is music. Which is one
way to one branch of modern music. Utility is a dull word, but it
may be borne in mind. The gadgets may also be borne in
mind. And so may that other horror of dehydrated journalism—
'gimmick'.

At once we may profitably turn to three works. To the *Sinfonia
Antartica* which, springing from the art of the cinema, has
references, at least, to utilitarianism: to the generally gay, extra-
vert symphonies (two in all) of Malcolm Arnold, which, in the
best sense of the word, are characterized by an up-to-dateness in
the employment of instruments that in itself is engaging: to the
just post-war *Sinfonietta* of Poulenc, in which the gimmickery
(as in so much of Poulenc) lies in a nervously persistent *insouciance*.

Whether these represent 'great music' is neither here nor there.
Mozart and Haydn proved that one way to immortality was by
leaving 'greatness' to look after itself. Which is an invitation to
the reader to form his own tastes; assuming that he has an en-
quiring turn of mind, and will look about for material on which
taste may be formed. Copland, Milhaud, Prokofiev, Shostakovich, Barber, Harris, Britten, Malipiero, Rubbra are contemporary composers (with symphonies composed within the
last decade) in addition to the three already mentioned who set
no problems which cannot be solved by the listener whose experience of music is reasonably wide. There are, of course, others:
but there are many which should not be altogether unfamiliar to
concert-goer or discophile and which may be recommended as
intelligible to all save the tone-deaf. It is, however, one of the
less satisfying facets of modernity that those who are prob-
lematic are seized upon by the *avante-garde* critic as being more
profitable that those who are not.

¶ THE TWELVE-NOTE ROW · Impressionist; cubist; surrealist;
abstractionist; realist: the visitor to the Tate Gallery picks up the
terminology and assumes it a necessary aid to the appreciation of
pictures. The earnest music student settles down to a similar
jargon: neo-classical; neo-Baroque; neo-Romantic; dodecaphonic.
Thus music is systematized, and, unless he has listened to the

sage counsel of Dr Rubbra, the young composer tends to become a member of one of the factions. Thus is explained a habit of addressing a select rather than a general audience, and this is where the innocent music-lover, unaware of the cliques, comes unstuck. Yet it is not quite as easy as that. As may be seen in respect of dodecaphony.

Dodecaphonic once was a magic word. It is, I believe, not so any more. But the listener might as well become acquainted with the dodecaphonic principle, for its influence has so spread that few composers are unaware of its possibilities. The basis of classical and romantic music was tonality. The late Romantic composers, in search of 'expression', blew tonal principles sky-high by a tendency, illustrated by Liszt, by Wagner, by Franck, by Mahler, never to stay in a particular key if it was possible to get out of it. Thus when Schoenberg (the prophet of dodeca-phony) came to maturity some fifty years ago he promulgated the thesis (enlarged upon by his disciples) that tonality was finished; that 'harmony', as it was understood in the nineteenth century, was a dead end.

Clearly no creative artist of integrity destroys without rebuild-ing. Thus in place of the former major-minor tonal system came the thesis that the twelve notes of the chromatic scale, from which music must necessarily be constructed until such times as quarter-tones become generally appreciated, were each of equal im-portance. Not only that, they were the only begetters of musical development.

Accordingly one arranged the twelve notes in a particular way and that was the basic melody. Necessarily the notes were ordered rhythmically. The 'note-row' thus formed could be treated canonically. It could be inverted (i.e. played upside-down). It could be treated *cancrizans* (i.e. from back to front). And the notes could be piled on top of each other to form chordal groups. There is a lot more to it than that, but those who would pursue the matter further are referred to *Composition with Twelve Notes related only to one another*,[1] by Joseph Rufer, who was a pupil of Schoenberg.

[1] Trans. Humphrey Searle (Rockcliff), 1955

Music written according to this system may be moving (see Berg's Violin concreto, or the same composer's *Lulu*, or Humphrey Searle's *The Riverrun*, based on the conclusion of James Joyce's *Finnegan's Wake*); it may be only 'interesting'—which is the case in respect of much of the music of Ernst Křenek; it may be eccentric as lately displayed in the work of the German Giselher Klebe. Dodecaphonic music appeals to the eye; rather less, in its most stringent forms, to the ear.

'The learned academic devices in which the dodecaphonists indulge', wrote Charles Koechlin, the French composer, 'are not difficult to write; what is difficult is to make them interesting as *music*.' Accepting that as axiomatic—that dodecaphony alone may appear sterile—it is only just to add that its cult has served a larger purpose. For composers may now no longer take form, and technique in general, for granted. The 'classical' symphonic form; the dramatics of Beethoven; the emotionalism of the Romantics; the folkiness of the nationalists; made it quite possible to compose an *efficient* symphony (in that it filled half an hour or more with cohesive utterance), in which lack of purpose or of genuine imagination was quite disguised. At present, without the formal restriction which bound down such a composer, for example, as Bax (whose symphonies are unjustly ignored), the composer is a free agent. But he may only depend on himself. Thus no two contemporary symphonies are quite alike. Which should, at least, inspire the listener with the idea that there is a good deal that is interesting to be discovered.

❡ NEW SONORITIES · Economy is clearly an artistic virtue, and it succeeds opulence. After the large works scored for vast orchestras which were the norm of the pre-first-war period came more modest pieces. So Webern's symphony employed clarinet, bass clarinet, two horns, harp, and strings without double bass. And melody again asserted its independence. So we may quote Milhaud—'What I wanted was to eliminate all non-essential links, and to provide each instrument with an independent melodic line or tonality. In this case [*L'Enfant Prodigue*], polytonality is no longer a matter of chords, but of the encounter of lines. . . . I was attracted by the unusual quality of small groups of instruments, and embarked on a series of *Petites Symphonies* for seven or eight different instruments. . . . The audience did not seem to object to the sound of my music, but ignorant or forgetful of the fact that in the days of Monteverdi the word "symphony" was sometimes used to denote a single page of instrumental music, it expected to hear a huge work played by a huge orchestra and was shocked by the brevity of my piece.' With a Gallic logic and a sense of humour Milhaud carried his theories —or those of his contemporaries—to their natural conclusions; with, as he records, sometimes provoking results. A considerable, but not a great, composer he is not of universal significance in the way in which Stravinsky is.

¶ IGOR STRAVINSKY (b. 1882) · Stravinsky continues to experiment, to the extent that his works of the mid-1950's are according to the dodecaphonic rule-book. But his influence hitherto has depended (a) on his superb realization of music apt for ballet and (b) on his revivification of classical principles. And here one may turn to the symphony in C, written in 1940. This has been called 'the crystallization of a symphony: transparent, cold, hard as a diamond, aloof, and pure'.

In normal four-movement plan (the work lasts only for twenty-eight minutes) the music has many links with the eighteenth century. It is absolute—quite devoid of realistic association. Its figuration, especially in the outer movements, is formal. The expansion of the figuration is through rhythmic and contrapuntal development—thus the harmonic structure is of secondary importance.

The modest score (Brahms's orchestra) is so laid out that each instrumental line is tonally independent. The first movement is, broadly speaking, according to the 'sonata form' precept, with exposition, development, recapitulation. (How much easier it would be if we could adopt the Aristotelean 'beginning, middle, and end' for symphonic discussion.) In the second movement, *larghetto concertante*, two ideas combine. Traditionally the classical slow movement allowed free play to melodic invention. And so it is here; but now the melodies are instrumental rather than vocal. This is a factor to be borne in mind in relation to contemporary

music in general. Secondly a number of instruments are conspicuous at the same time. Thus oboe, flute, and clarinet for the
first twelve bars; then oboe and violin; then the strings alone;
then oboe and first violin again. . . . It is the *lines* of sound, each
growing from its predecessor and each in some way allied to the
melodic gambits of the first movement which run through the
whole symphony, which capture the attention. The lines of
sound and the rhythms. Stravinsky's rhythmic invention is a
study in itself. It is perhaps sufficient to say that even in his most
'neo-classic' period he never forgot that he was a composer of
ballet. In the present instance turn to the diversionary character
of the third movement.

One may acclimatize oneself to this side of Stravinsky (also
exposed in the *Symphony in three movements* of 1945) by way of the
ballet-suite *Pulcinella*—in which the composer disports himself
with tunes from Pergolesi. But there is the other side of Stravinsky: the 'Russian'. Splendour of scoring, enthusiasm, elemental
vigour: these are the qualities in *The Fire Bird* and *Petrushka*,
which even now must appear remarkable by reason of their
essential—not fortuitous—modernity. The apotheosis of this style
is in the *Symphony of Psalms*.

The *Symphony of Psalms* is remarkable not only because in it the
words (of parts of Psalms XXXVIII and XXXIX and the whole
of Psalm CL) are 'set' effectively—in that their significance is
heightened by music—but because the chorus is integrated within
the ensemble. This indeed is truly a choral symphony, but also,
as in the Monteverdi or Schütz manner, a *sinfonia sacra*. Melodically austere, the symphony is given direction by splendid and
striking colouring (the orchestration is detailed on p. 30) and by
pointed rhythms.

It is sometimes said that Stravinsky lacks 'feeling'; that his
attitude is too objective. Study carefully the second psalm—a
masterpiece of 'linear' music—and notice how the opening *fugato*
leads ineluctably to the entry of the soprano voices with the
words 'Expectans expectavi Dominum'.

So far we find in the music of today four prominent impulses.
Tonality is not what it was; melody is of greater significance

than formerly, but its origins may be instrumental rather than vocal; rhythmic energy can no longer contain itself within the metres that served our grandfathers; and instrumental sonorities present novel scope. Further there is a strong movement towards 'absolute' music, which is summed up in symphony. There are some composers who keep one foot within the traditions familiar to conventional audiences—such, perhaps, is Shostakovich and other recent Soviet composers. There are others who go forward towards the future, but not out of step with the present. Such a one is Peter Racine Fricker, whose two symphonies are amongst the most notable achievements in post-war British music.

❮ PETER RACINE FRICKER (b. 1920) · Fricker's first symphony, dedicated to the Koussevitzky Foundation (the generosity of Koussevitzky to modern composers and the part played by the Boston Symphony Orchestra, of which he was conductor, cannot be disregarded in any survey of contemporary music), was first performed at the Cheltenham Festival in 1950, under the direction of Sir John Barbirolli.

At once one is impressed by Fricker's confidence in his themes. A slow introduction unfolds two statements, the one in the trombones, the other in the flutes. The introduction leads to a high climax, in which rhythmic factors become more marked and in which the whole orchestra is involved. The function of the piano —to harden the rhythmic and melodic ranges—should be noted. Then follows the first movement proper. At the outset the principal subject is allied with a subsidiary figure in a fugal exposition. The growth of this material into a monumental first movement— large in scope but not long—is achieved by a fine contrapuntal technique (note how the flute tune from the introduction is blended into the texture, and how the initial trombone motiv returns in the final passage), by a sense of climax, by an ability to instrumentate without digression. Fricker uses his instruments purposefully and not because they 'sound nice'. But this is no single-track mind.

The slow movement is intense without being picturesque or melodramatic; serious without solemnity; profound but not obscure. One would say tuneful; for the themes are memorable and far-reaching. Note how the first tune of the violins (accompanied by muted trombones and bass drum) carries throughout the movement, throwing off fresh growth as it proceeds. Note, too, how it is repeated at the end of the movement, by flute and with the rhythmic outline modified, against the bass drum.

Fricker is a mature composer in the sense that he treats his public seriously. This has led some to criticize him for being a too serious writer. I do not think the listener need feel that this is so, if he is prepared to dispense with adventitious aids to musical progress. Fricker is not a 'programmatic' composer, and the strength of his music lies precisely in the fact that programmes would not in any way explicate his thought.

At the same time there is no lack of beauty (see the slow movement of the first symphony); nor, as the robust 'Tableau and Dance', which is the third movement, shows, of humour. Here one senses an English ancestry—for so, thirty years ago, did Vaughan Williams similarly exercise himself in the robust scherzo of the *Pastoral Symphony*. In the final movement, which is essentially contrapuntal in development, there is masterly orchestration which deserves the closest attention. Notice how there is nothing superfluous and then how the economy leads to new and sometimes fantastic combinations and contrasts of timbre. The passage from [12] might be instanced, where two trumpets are placed against a cutting theme in the violas and above a persistent drum pedal, to be joined shortly by flutes, clarinets, and horn in a manner reminiscent of an eighteenth-century concerto.

And this is where Fricker joins with Stravinsky in taking hold of traditional values—but from an earlier style of western musical tradition than is sometimes familiar to the rank and file. So much may serve as introduction to Fricker's other music (of which there is by now a significant corpus): and especially to the second symphony, which was commissioned by the City of Liverpool for the Festival of Britain.

❡ THE COMPOSER AND SOCIETY · From such discussion two points worthy of emphasis emerge. The first concerns the composer. The contemporary composer of symphonic stature is less open to compromise than his nineteenth-century predecessor.

And this implies that the listener is likely to be treated with respect—as one who is willing to make the effort to come to terms. We do not always 'understand' what is being said, but, aware that what is being said has been seriously considered, we listen again.

The second point concerns patronage. In earlier times the composer depended for some part of his livelihood on a private patron. Now corporate bodies begin to take their place: the organizing committees of Festivals (the Venice *biennale* for instance); the city (Alan Bush composed a *Nottingham Symphony* for a civic occasion); the state (Milhaud's third symphony—*Hymnus Ambrosianus*—was an extension of a commission to write a *Te Deum* to celebrate the liberation of France in 1945). So far as patronage by the state is concerned none has done more than the government of the U.S.S.R.

This brings us to a particular problem of our time. We—say the officers of the State to the composer—will feed you, and house you, and give you holiday facilities; in return for which you will compose as and when required. So far so good. But there might follow (as in Russia in 1938) conditions. Your music must not be contaminated with bourgeois ways; it must express the will of the people, faith in a particular and exclusive tradition; it must be simple and intelligible to the common man. Kabalevsky, Khatchaturian, Miaskovsky, Prokofiev (a repentant deviationist), Shostakovich, are principal among those who have both benefited and suffered from the extremes of latter-day Russian ideological enthusiasm.

❡ DIMITRI SHOSTAKOVICH (b. 1906) · Of these composers Shostakovich is the best known and the most talented. In all his music we can read the personality of the composer, and in so doing relate him to the Romantic tradition of which he is one of the latest exponents. Thus the symphonies of Shostakovich have a chequered record. The first, first performed in 1926, was acclaimed at once as a masterpiece of virtuoso orchestration, while its energy and spontaneity, its tunefulness, gained immediate popularity. There followed three failures—*To October* (1927), *May Day* (1929), and a fourth symphony that was not even performed. The fifth symphony came in 1936, when the composer was out of official favour. But its success both at home and abroad was immense: a powerful and spacious work. Two years later the sixth symphony broke with traditional design by commencing with the slow movement. This, large and emotional, is followed by a *scherzo* with sardonic characteristics and a very rhythmic *presto* as finale.

The succeeding three symphonies (1941, 1942, 1945) form a wartime trilogy. The seventh symphony, indeed, was written in Leningrad in 1941 during the siege of the city by the German armies. 'I planned this work', said Shostakovich, 'as an expression of the majestic ideas of the patriotic war. Neither savage raids, German planes, nor the grim atmosphere of the beleaguered city could hinder the flow of ideas. I worked with an inhuman intensity I have never before reached.'

Neither in music nor in poetry do hot emotion and high aspiration necessarily result in great art. Ten years ago Shostakovich's seventh symphony was played throughout the (allied) world. But not now. Nor are the ideologically proper eighth and ninth symphonies. The tenth symphony (1953) has found perhaps better reception in the western world than in the U.S.S.R. A long first movement, which Hugh Ottaway finds reminiscent of Nielsen, is notable for its breadth and deliberation, and for the brilliant use of a very large orchestra. This, the best of the movements, is followed by a brief *scherzo*—in which the 'fierceness' of the Slav is sublimated—an *allegretto*, and a two-part finale—*Andante* and *allegro*.

The music of Shostakovich is that of a willing, eager mind, and is technically highly accomplished. It does, however, look backwards rather than forwards. In short—and this is what might be expected—it compromises with ideas which in themselves are unnecessary to music. I am not unwilling to believe that the 'spirit of the age' communicates itself to works of art: but it will not materialize when sought for.

❡ TENDENCIES IN U.S.A. · However, good citizenship has many symphonies to its credit. In Russia practically every symphony is citizenly, and therefore basically romantic, and obviously inclined to be non-modern. And something similar happens in the U.S.A., where numerous Foundations and Trusts, as well as the progressiveness of some of the leading orchestras, make the publication and performance of new music considerably easier than is the case in Britain.

Samuel Barber, a magnificent manipulator of music according to classical and pre-classical formulas, wrote his second symphony in 1944 after service in the United States Army Air Force. Hence the second movement sports an electrical instrument (made specially) which 'simulates the sound of a radio beam giving a code message to a pilot. . . .' Henry Cowell's fourth symphony is a collection of hymn tunes. Morton Gould's symphonies, on the other hand (as those of numerous other American composers), borrow from jazz idiom, which is crossed with fugue and passa-caglia forms to give a durable finish. Howard Hanson, a deliberate composer, with a hankering after the long-ago, is given to com-memorative symphonies. Of such elements is 'American' music often compounded.

But there is—and Randall Thompson notes the distinction—much music, of wider scope and concern—'music by Americans'. Thus the finely graven, if conservative, symphonic essays of Randall Thompson himself, Paul Creston, and William Schuman; the glittering scores of Copland and Piston, two composers who understand to the full the virtuoso propensities of the modern symphony orchestra of which that from Boston is a notable example.

❡ ROMANTIC AND RELIGIOUS IMPULSES · The technical effi-ciency of the contemporary composer is sometimes misleading. So exhilarating can virtuosity be that music itself may be lost. There is, of course, nothing very new about this, but the favoured position of the 'symphony orchestra' in public esteem, and the conductor cult, may at times leave us wondering whether the composer is not regarded as the servant of his aides rather than their master. To what extent this is the case is a matter of indivi-dual judgment. On the whole, however, the most colourful works, which employ the largest available orchestra, tend to look backwards towards the high summer of efficient Romanticism.

D

Romanticism is always with us. And if one selects judiciously it is possible to cajole oneself into believing that the nineteenth century has in no way yet relaxed its hold on the public ear.

Organized religion is a less effective force in common affairs than formerly. But the need for spiritual exercise has not been (and presumably never will be) cancelled by the rigorous doctrines of contemporary science and philosophy. Music furnishes one opportunity for spiritual recreation and it is a notable feature of concert-going that it is now regarded as one of the solemnities. (A too solemn attitude, in my view, vitiates our understanding of, say, Haydn and Mozart.)

Abstract music, influenced by new tonal and rhythmic techniques, to which some attention has been paid, affiliates itself with progressive tendencies in thought; and it is no accident that such music commends itself to scientists, mathematicians, and engineers. Such music as that of the later Stravinsky, of Fricker, of Rawsthorne, of Pijper (the Dutch symphonist), of Holmboe (a Danish composer whose works are now beginning to establish themselves outside Scandinavia), in itself will often reflect the climate of advanced contemporary thought. Thus modernity is real rather than apparent.

Graphic music (the 'Leningrad' symphony being a case in point) will give an appearance of up-to-dateness. But topicality has nothing to do with essential modernity.

A reading of history (whether musical or otherwise) often helps understanding of situations. The present position of music is in many ways similar to that which obtained in the seventeenth century. Then the antitheses were similarly represented with some violence: the *nuove musiche* on the one hand, the traditional, but persistent, mediaeval on the other; monody *versus* polyphony; scale *versus* mode; instruments *versus* voices; music for music's sake *versus* music-with-a-purpose (i.e. 'sacred music').

The religious impulse transferred itself from church to secular music some time during the Romantic period. That this transferred authority is still respected is evident in many modern symphonic works. There may be instanced Britten's *Sinfonia da Requiem*—a series of reflections on three sections of the Mass

(I *Lacrymosa*, II *Dies Irae*, III *Requiem Aeternam*); Vaughan Williams's fifth symphony in D major, which is intimately associated with his *Pilgrim's Progress*; Paul Creston's third symphony, of which the individual movements are entitled: I *The Nativity*, II *The Crucifixion*, III *The Resurrection* and in which plainsong motivs are quoted; the symphonies of Edmund Rubbra, of which the distinguishing quality comes directly from a re-presentation of mediaeval feeling in more or less modern terms; and those of Malipiero.

IV. The Symphony Yesterday

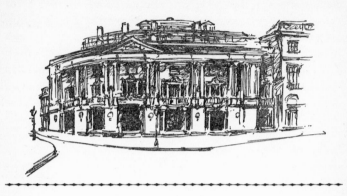

❡ RALPH VAUGHAN WILLIAMS (b. 1872) · It is more than a little unfair to suggest that any music by Vaughan Williams is behind the times. But his reputation was established so long ago that it is convenient to look through his symphonies—starting at the wrong end—to see how the present has emerged from the past. There is, says a recent critic, nothing new in the eighth symphony, nothing that Vaughan Williams has not said before. Yet—considering the diversity of critical opinion expressed after the first performance, in Manchester by the Hallé Orchestra on 2 May 1956, this does not sound entirely convincing.

In the eighth symphony Vaughan Williams is in teasing mood. If variations (see the *Passacaglia* of the fifth symphony, or the finale of Dvořák's fourth) may serve as the finale of a symphony, why not for a first movement? So here the first movement is a series of seven variations. But this is not the end of the matter; for there is no theme from which the variations extend. Or if there was it was discarded, thereby providing a new 'enigma'. When it is considered this quiddity really is a typical gesture. Economy, cutting down; those are the contemporary lodestars. And what could be more economical than dispensing with a

formality—for that, in truth, is what the initial 'theme' of variation form had become. Symphonic variations (from Franck to
Ian Hamilton) have proved a fascination to composers anxious to
conduct themselves with some formal propriety: and symphonic
variations will well describe this movement of Vaughan Williams.

However, there are three further movements: a *Scherzo alla
Marcia*, for wind instruments; a *Cavatina* for strings; and a
Toccata. In passing one notices how aptly the movements are
titled—especially the last, for the literal rendering of *toccata* as
'touched' justifies the character of the movement. 'Besides full
strings and wind', writes the composer in his informative and
diverting programme note, '[it] commandeers all the available
hitting instruments which can make definite notes, including
glockenspiel, celesta, xylophone, vibraphone, tubular bells and
tuned gongs.'

The melodic character of the work is familiar. The folk tune,
or plainsong quality, the featured fourths (since the symphony in
F minor these are often modified by diminution or augmenta-
tion), the sturdy and explicit rhythms are as in earlier works. The
harmonic quality is as ever diatonic and gritty. The development
of material in *fugato* fashion (see the *Scherzo*) lines up with similar
working out as in the fourth symphony. Up to this point the
suggestion that there is nothing new is true enough. It is in the
exploration of sonorities, the transformation of essential symphonic style (the composer's note shows how traditional the lay-
out really is), in the siting of familiar patterns that the element of
the new lies.

If this is an up-to-date classical essay (abstract music patterned
according to precedent) its predecessor was a full-blown Romantic piece. The *Sinfonia Antartica*, written in 1953, was formulated
from some of the themes which belonged to the film *Scott of the
Antarctic*. There are five movements: *Prelude*, *Scherzo*, *Landscape*
(*lento*), *Intermezzo*, and *Epilogue*. And each of the movements is
preceded by a text; from Shelley, Psalm 104, Coleridge, Donne,
and *Captain Scott's Last Journal*. All this literary background recalls the nineteenth century. But the character of nineteenth-
century Romantic, atmospheric music, was generous and warm.

Here is the obverse. An odd, austere score, with remarkable details of orchestration, especially in respect of the percussion department. For, as in Mahler's 'Tragic' symphony, those instruments are employed to lower rather than to heighten the emotional temperature.

The sixth symphony, in E minor, was written between 1944 and 1947. Together with the fourth, in F minor (1935), this shows the composer absolutely occupied in symphonic design without any direct reference to externals. Through all the works the elements of the style remain constant. That is, relationship can be established with such other works as the *Tallis Fantasia*, *Flos Campi*, *Riders to the Sea*, the *Magnificat*, *Five Tudor Portraits*—to take works of widely different orders—which suggests that song is at the root of the comprehensive style. And this is a line which the listener may profitably follow. It is in the vocal, or choral, character (derived from the study of folk song and liturgical music of the sixteenth century) of his symphonies that the most original contribution of Vaughan Williams to modern music may be found.

If this implies that there should be apparent a palpable lyricism look at the fifth symphony in D major (1943), at the *Pastoral Symphony* (1922), or at the *Sea Symphony* (1910) which is a full-scale and full-blooded choral symphony.

There remains the *London Symphony* (1920), which is programme music—but without a programme. That is to say the tunes (in which the work is fertile) are not specifically descriptive—as in Elgar's *Cockaigne* overture. At the same time the whole symphony is evocative of familiar phases of London life. It was Vaughan Williams himself who said that this could better be called a 'symphony by a Londoner' rather than a 'London Symphony'; an anticipation of the phrase concerning American music by Randall Thompson to which reference is made on p. 49.

The *London Symphony* was first performed at the Queen's Hall, London, on 27 March 1914, and the conductor was Geoffrey Toye. The circumstances of this performance—at a concert promoted by Bevis Ellis, a wealthy young amateur of the arts who aspired to putting English symphonic music on its feet by his patronage—serves to show how difficult it was in those far-off days for English symphonists to gain a hearing. Unless, as was the case with Elgar, they were championed by a distinguished foreign conductor. That Elgar's genius flowered so completely during the Edwardian era was due in large measure to the efforts on his behalf of Hans Richter.

¶ EDWARD ELGAR (1857–1934) · It is a quite startling experience to hear side by side the second symphony of Elgar and the *London Symphony* of Vaughan Williams, realizing that only three years divided their production. For the music of the latter has that quality of aggression, of bluntness, that still strikes the ear as 'modern'; indeed the vocabulary of the *London* is recognizable as the vocabulary of the eighth symphony, which is nothing behind the times in 1957. On the other hand the second symphony of Elgar sounds its kinship with Dvořák, with Schumann, with Beethoven.

That this work has been so long in reaching the L.P. catalogues is a disgrace. By any standards it is a great work—generous, open-hearted, brilliant. Its inner history is fascinating.

As a young man Elgar aspired (for he was a nineteenth-century Romantic through and through) one day to compose a *sinfonia eroica*. He had his subject ready in the career of General Gordon. With Gordon in mind Elgar commenced a character study (c.f. *Falstaff*, which was in mind almost as early) in 1898. But the project went no further than a miscellany of jottings in a sketch-book. Six years later the opportunity for a symphony seemed to offer itself in the Elgar Festival at Convent Garden Theatre. And more sketches accrued. But circumstances turned against a symphony on that occasion, and those who looked for a symphony from Elgar had to be content with the overture—in name, but much more a symphonic poem—*In the South*. As a matter of interest the overture is in the same key as the symphonic sketches and it also is—according to its literary annotations—a 'heroic' work.

One of the many unanswered—and unanswerable—questions relating to Elgar is why, when in 1907 he finally began to work earnestly at a symphony, he set aside the already considerable sketches and started afresh. For there are no traces of the A flat symphony before that date.

Part of the answer lies, probably, in the theme which commences and dominates the symphony. Here, said Elgar, having chanced upon the idea, is a melody worthy of a symphony. As nearly always the music was for him indicative of extra-musical ideas. In this he shows his proper Romantic affiliation. A quotation from a letter from the composer to his friend Walford Davies gives all the clue that is necessary. 'There is', he wrote, 'no pro-gramme beyond a wide experience of human life with a great charity (love) and a *massive* hope in the future.' Play the opening bars of the symphony, grandly set in two-part counterpoint. Now turn to the last movement, where this principal theme stirs anew at [129]; and next to [146], where it reaches its ultimate ennoblement. Go back to the first movement after [5], where tonality is obscure and rhythm instinct with trouble.

It is not an easy march towards the millenium. But there are refuges by the wayside. Such is the *adagio* (few composers have written slow movements of greater serenity and eloquence). This movement is based on the theme of the *scherzo*, which stands second in the symphony. For those whose immediate concern is orchestration both the Elgar symphonies are a mine of delight. Apart from the passages for full orchestra, which are fewer than some of his detractors would have us believe, where the richness of tone is remarkable, attention may be drawn to the subtleties: such as lie in the woodwind and high strings from [29] to [31]; from [91] to the end of the *scherzo*, as instruments disappear from the score; between [98] and [100] in the slow movement, where clarinet and solo violin intertwine.

At the first performance, under Richter in Manchester, the enthusiasm of the audience was unbounded. They rose to applaud at the end of the slow movement. And when the first London performance was due people (many of whom could not get into Queen's Hall) fought for tickets with as much zest as was shown in respect of those for the visit of the Bolshoi Ballet Company in 1956.

The second symphony in E flat was heard for the first time at the London Music Festival of 1911. More opulent, less sensitive, than its predecessor it appeared as a Laureate's work. It bore the inscription 'Dedicated to the Memory of His late Majesty King Edward VII', and the slow movement (restored to its traditional place) is as a funeral march. One may well wonder what the third movement, a quippish rondo, has to do with the 'subject', until one realizes that it is a characteristically personal interpolation: Elgar himself, and against an Italian landscape—for many of his middle-period ideas were stimulated by his Italian journeys.

At least two fairly substantial parts of the second symphony were in being for years before its completion. And this is where we return to the sketches of 1904. For it was these which produced that part of the slow movement which begins at [74] and the second subject of the last movement.

It is easy to be wise after the event, and to suggest that Elgar's symphonies are episodic works upon which an artificial unity has been imposed. But methods of composition are various. If Elgar appears, in some aspects, as a *picaresque* composer (he had a great affection for the novelists of the eighteenth century) that is part of his distinction; and in any case he was too practical to continue—as does Mahler, with whom some comparisons are valid—beyond audience endurance.

The two major English symphonists, so far indisputably established, are Elgar and Vaughan Williams—to whom English composers as a whole owe a great debt for their persistence against odds. (Consider the crying-down of English opera, the effect of this on composers, and then compare the happier situation of instrumental music.)

❡ ARNOLD BAX (1883–1953) · In the first half of this century there were some notable casualties among English symphonies. Granville Bantock, once one of the white hopes of native music; Joseph Holbrooke—whose attempts to express Edgar Allan Poe through symphonic poems were striking; Havergal Brian, a self-taught composer of some power and great single-mindedness; and Arnold Bax, occur in this melancholy connection.

Why the seven symphonies of Bax should have been sunk without trace is a complete mystery. Or do we have a quota (as in

the case of films) so that a programme must contain one part
classical, two parts Romantic, one part early twentieth-century
continental, one part British or American? Bax lived, perhaps, at
the wrong time. He believed, quite simply, that music should be
'beautiful'. And such a plain-and-easy thesis was unacceptable in
the post-first war years. His music has its affinities with Elgar but
also with Delius. Sometimes Sibelius and Vaughan Williams are
detectable. One particular source of inspiration, however, was
the scenery of Connemara, the poetry of Yeats and the culture of
the Irish renascence—of wonder. It is not without significance
that Bax's symphonies are all cast in something of the same mood
of pessimism; and that, except for the sixth symphony, none have
scherzos. In orchestral colouring, however, these are as attractive
as any works in the English catalogue. But since *The Garden of
Faud*, *Tintagel*, and *The Song of the Faery Hills*, have all this—and
less of the obscurity which envelops the symphonic themes in not
always vocal contours and in perplexing rhythms—the symphonies are ignored.

⟦ WILLIAM WALTON (b. 1902) · Elgar, Vaughan Williams, and
Bax—all in a sense 'local' composers—were aware of one contemporary symphonist of undisputed power and with influence
beyond his own country: Jean Sibelius. Both Vaughan Williams
and Bax dedicated their fifth symphonies to Sibelius. And his
mark is on the most outstanding of English symphonies of the
between-war years: that of William Walton, composed in 1935.
Compare (bearing in mind that thirty years separated the two
works) the opening of Sibelius's third symphony with that of
Walton's: terse, abundantly rhythmic, and spacious, but without
departing from an economy of timbre. Bernard Shore perceives
the imaginative connection when he writes of Walton's commencement thus: 'Walton plants B flat deep in virgin soil; it is a
tree of a forest; and we are at once held by the strength of the
roots. The tonality is immediately clear, and there is a grand
feeling of space and power in the wide lay-out of the score, clear
in its sustained harmony of a bare fifth, agitated by the strings.'

Later in the same essay we read (of the passage in the first
movement between [17] and [18]) 'In a page taken from the book

of Sibelius, woodwind, strings, and trumpets suddenly concentrate on one note, and hammer out a terrific series of syllables, driving home that one change of note that the oboe makes in his opening phrases or first theme' (see bars 13–17 of first movement). Instances of this kind of intensified scoring of a single line may be found—though with differences of tone pressure—throughout Sibelius; especially in the first movement of the second symphony, and the finales of symphonies 4 and 5. Walton also shares with Sibelius an austerity of melodic outline. There is nothing ingratiating about the patterns that unfold in the first movement up to figure [11]; but there is character.

And that was what was felt twenty years ago (and should be felt now) when the symphony was new. An elemental work—see how it proceeds along the path shown by the bare fifths, as in the Choral Symphony of Beethoven—with a rhythmic *élan* and a clarity of texture that was not at all usual in British music. As a study in rhythm the second movement *scherzo* is superb. *Presto con malizia* it is marked; which is the precise description of its temper. (The student might well study the passage between [57] and [73] to see how intimately associated are the ideas and their orchestral expression.) Yet it was not for nothing that Walton long ago declared his respect for Elgar—a respect that has borne some of the best post-Elgarian ceremonial music. The slow movement—*andante con malincolia*—is a romantic interlude, in which there is a mastery of string technique, a manipulation of texture, a nervous melodic outline that extends beyond personal thoughts, and a dynamic urge, that compel admiration for the fertility of imagination of the composer.

To write a final movement to match the first three was a problem which Walton found difficult to solve. In fact the first performance of the symphony, in December 1934, was of the first three movements only; the finale being heard, and therefore the complete symphony, a year later.

The finale comprises an introduction (the thematic material furnishing the melodic patterns of the whole movement), two fugal passages, separated by an episode [117], of more emotional quality, and a blazing epilogue. In this, in which the music at last is firmly within the key of B flat, one is again aware of an Elgarian quality—*maestoso* taking the place of Elgar's *nobilmente*.

This symphony is a shattering experience. As compact with thought as a pamphlet by Swift, and as lucid in argument, it has also a degree of passion that recalls that master's *saeva indignatio*. And it promises to survive the passage of time. So can one composer say more in one symphony than others in a dozen. It is rare, however, for this to be achieved at the first attempt.

❡ JEAN SIBELIUS (b. 1865) · Some two or three composers, at most, in a generation become accepted as universal figures. Since the death of Brahms, Dvořák, and Tchaikovsky virtually only one composer has attained this rank by reason of his symphonic music: Jean Sibelius. And, for various reasons, his universality is no more than partial. For, while accepted as a classic in the Scandinavian countries, in Britain, Germany, and America, he is hardly recognized in the Latin countries. To say that his scores are cold and that the southerners prefer music with warmth, sounds, perhaps, too much like the beginning of a meteorologist's bulletin. Yet that is the sum of the case for and against.

Romantic symphonies continued to thrive, in an over-heated atmosphere, and it was apparent that ventilation was badly needed. So began 'modern' music (which has, however, shown certain tendencies to mistake draughts for fresh air). Sibelius, then, is the first modern symphonist. Yet he was no iconoclast. He took up where his predecessors left off; so that the first symphony, in E minor, has recollections of Tchaikovsky and Glazounov. It is obedient to the conventions of form, and the first and last movements are bound together by just such an introductory theme as Tchaikovsky might have envisaged. But Tchaikovsky would not have such a theme, in the first place for a solo clarinet above a drum roll, nor in the second for the strings, in octaves, against the punctuating brass. Harmony, it is felt here, is no longer the discipline that it was.

Throughout the first symphony there is an awareness of instrumental sonorities that was quite new in 1901. Lines rather than masses of sound predominate; woodwind is independent of string—notice the particularly Sibelian effect of woodwind rising out of the score in progressions of thirds; long pedal notes in the bass give an amplitude to the upper writing; contrasts of tone are abrupt and refreshing; there is, too, a new rhythmic energy that is, at the same time, flexible. And the melodic idiom is taciturn.

When he composed his first symphony, at the age of thirty-four or thereabouts, Sibelius was a considerable figure in Finnish music, with such works as *En Saga*, *Karelia*, the four legends from the *Kalevala*, and *Finlandia* already well known. In each of these Sibelius showed the direction he would take: towards a musical style which, independent of folk music idioms, should enshrine the qualities of Finnish legend and history.

His studies in Berlin and Vienna had been brief, and with lesser rather than greater masters, so that he was compelled to evolve his own style. In this, as in his early profession as violin player, Sibelius was akin to Elgar. The comparison is apt, for the Finnish quality of the one, and the English quality of the other (both unmistakable, so it seems, to foreigners) spring from inner conviction and not from such adventitious aids as folk-tunes may afford. One may, of course, be secretly convinced that the slow movements of the second, third, and fourth symphonies, for example, contain folk-songs thinly disguised; but that only goes to show to what extent a great composer may achieve authority in a bardic capacity. More almost than any other composer of modern times Sibelius is identified with his country: largely through the character of his music, but partly through the know-ledge that from 1897 onwards he was able to live supported by a grant from the government. British governments find it more economical to award 'honours'.

The seven symphonies of Sibelius cover the first quarter of the century, the last, together with *Tapiola*, dating from 1924–5, and it is difficult to find a sequence of symphonies by any other com-poser which has followed such a direct and logical course. It is symptomatic of the general tendency of significant twentieth-century art to pursue the ideals of clarity and understatement that Sibelius's symphonies should have progressively grown slighter in physique, until the last, of one movement, is of but twenty minutes' duration, and scored for a relatively small orchestra (classical, but for four horns and three trumpets).

In the process of symphonic simplification Sibelius turned away, after the first symphony, from the cross-fertilization of movements with thematic mottoes. Thus his movements are self-contained units. In general, except for the seventh and third symphonies (in this there is no slow movement), the four-movement plan sufficed; but the inner organization of the movements is apart from the conventional—and 'academic'—formulae. Altogether Sibelius's movements are closer-knit than hitherto, and in place of long 'subjects' (which are only present in the first symphony) he employs pregnant germ-motivs which are fitted together in mosaic fashion.

The second symphony, the most genial of the set, ranks understandably high in public esteem, and I see no reason why Sibelians should take to apologizing for the work. But hope and faith are out of favour; and so long as they are the second symphony will hardly escape critical depreciation as a middle-brow's *Finlandia*. Of somewhat similar mood is the fifth symphony in E flat, which runs next to the second in popularity.

It was when studying Bax's third and Sibelius's fifth symphonies side by side (they are both in the same key) that the individuality of Sibelius stood out most vividly. There are some superficial resemblances. Bax is not without grimness—but it is, on the whole, an aspect of life accepted with resignation. He runs aggressive motivs through the texture of his first movement, and employs his trumpets and trombones trenchantly. But he turns away from the subject under discussion—often to experiment with some new and always delightful business of scoring. Against this diffuseness Sibelius is relentless. There is no divagation, never a note more than is necessary to the argument.

In the first movement of the E flat symphony 'tunes' are nonexistent. There are pregnant, even dogmatic, statements as brief as they are powerful. And it is evident that the orchestration is directed towards strength rather than grace. One look at the scoring of the first movement will show with what economy,

even brusqueness, the effects are contrived. To look for the traditional three-section outline of the movement is relatively profit-
less. For 'development' sections, as such, were viewed with some
suspicion by Sibelius: no composer ever let less 'padding' into
his music.

Characteristically abrupt is the manner in which the *scherzo*
supervenes. There is no break between first and second movements and the contrast between the heroic and the bucolic (for
Sibelius recollects this aspect of life with a vivid sympathy, yet
with no hint of affectation) is strongly marked. From the felicities
of statement must be quoted the duet between trumpet and drums,
against a background of strings, at [D], with the subsequent
switch from E flat to B major; and the coming-up of a mist in
the strings at [G], through which points of melody and tone
colour show through.

In his slow movements (though the third movement of the
fifth symphony is not quite slow—being marked *andante mosso,
quasi allegretto*)—Sibelius has a reserve akin to that of Brahms.
Perhaps here it is in the formal presentation, for the virtual mono-
thematic character of the movement infers a strong intellectual
control of wayward emotion. Sibelius may be greatly moved—
as from his correspondence he often would appear to be—but he
is never facile in emotional expression. This is why his music may
often appear (as is the case with the fourth symphony) over re-
strained to those for whom music is essentially a cathartic
experience.

Spaciousness; reticence; firmness; mystery; reverence; a tragic
(in the Aristotelean sense) point of view; those are Sibelius's
characteristics. To what extent they appear to overlap qualities in
Finnish landscape or character is the measure of his nationalism.
What is more important than determining the indeterminable is
the realization that the essential virtues of Sibelius's symphonies
represented a new and original voice in music.

⁋ CARL NIELSEN (1865–1931) · While Sibelius (whose cause
was espoused fifty years ago by Sir Granville Bantock) has long
been accepted in England, his contemporary Carl Nielsen has
been much longer in arriving. Not, I think, that Nielsen—a Dane

—really has yet arrived. To hear his symphonies in the concert hall is a rare experience.

Nielsen is the greatest name in modern Danish music and regarded in relation to his country's music as are Grieg and Sibelius to theirs. His early music derived from that of Gade and Svendsen. Like them—and all other Scandinavian composers—he determined to fashion a style independent of the commonplaces of the German academic tradition. Thus the distinctive features of his style are an insistence on rhythm (c.f. opening of *Sinfonia Espansiva*), on the integrity of melody, on the true development of melody through counterpoint, on an extension of tonal possibilities (Nielsen was among the earliest polytonalists), and on the cultivation of new sonorities. A good introduction to the music of Nielsen is the fifth symphony; in which there is much 'pastoral' figuration evoking such landscapes as are described in his autobiography, and a toughness of character that emerges into the march motiv of the second movement. (There are only two movements in the symphony.)

This symphony was finished in 1922 and was therefore contemporary with the *Pastoral Symphony* of Vaughan Williams. There is something to be said for hearing the two symphonies side by side, if only to mark the similarities and differences. Here are two composers relieving music as a whole from the burden of outworn tradition and arriving independently at not entirely dissimilar conclusions. The listener must decide for himself in what way the one is Danish and the other English, but it may well be felt that there is after all something in environment which is communicable through music.

V. The Great Symphonist

❡ THE MARK OF GREATNESS · In the secular sphere two or three men have proved themselves indispensable to civilization. Among them Plato, Michelangelo, Shakespeare, and, without doubt, Beethoven. This is in no way to suggest that Beethoven is the 'greatest' of composers within the field of music itself, but rather that his influence through music has affected human understanding more than that of almost any other composer. It is indisputable that each of the nine symphonies is as significant now as when written—perhaps even more so—and so, so far as we may judge, it will continue. As with Beethoven so also is it with Shakespeare. To begin to understand either it is worth while examining this proposition: that the music of the one and the drama of the other is indestructible. Why is this?

The answer is commenced by Thomas Mann. For so he writes in *Death in Venice*: 'For an intellectual product of any value to exert an immediate influence which should also be deep and lasting it must rest on an inner harmony, yes, an affinity, between the personal destiny of its author and that of his contemporaries in general. Men do not know why they award fame to one work of art rather than another. Without being in the faintest degree connoisseurs, they think to justify the warmth of their commendations by discovering in it a hundred virtues, whereas the real ground for their applause is inexplicable—it is sympathy.'

Biography is no part of our present concern, but reference to any of the standard biographies will give a lamentable picture; of the misunderstood genius, the world against him. In general, perhaps, Beethoven as man comes off better than he deserved; for it is difficult to escape the conclusion that some of his misfortunes were his own responsibility. Further, it is apparent that the thesis of the artist against the Philistines (see Schumann, in whom it had its fullest expression) was part of the mood of the age. But—and this is the remarkable feature—Beethoven never lost his belief that there were glories yet to come. So his symphonic career moved ineluctably towards the ninth symphony.

There is a division between Beethoven's life and the expression of his work. With few exceptions he did not love men—or women; but that he loved humanity is self-evident. So his symphonies do not illustrate one life—in the sense that Mahler's do—but universal life. You and I find ourselves within the music; now of the second, now of the eighth symphonies; at other times of the others. Our feeling is that the music bears personal significance. We are aware of the inner harmony, the affinity, the sympathy of which Mann speaks. This indelible quality has not been revealed in the fullness of time, but it was there at once. Beethoven, a child of the new age, understood the mood of his own time, transmuted it into music, and thereby showed its permanence.

Life is simpler than we make it. There is polarity: of love and hate, of peace and war, of tranquillity and action, of word and deed. But there are hidden complexities, for fear may lie behind hope, and moods may change against expectation. And there are reserves of emotional and intellectual power to defy the laws of probability. All this is mystery, unless fortified with a faith. Belonging to an age which disbelieved before it believed Beethoven's spiritual pilgrimage was hard, but towards the end was the great *Missa Solennis*, one of those documents which leaves no more to be said.

❡ AIMS · By all means accept Beethoven's music as it is, as 'absolute' music; but bear in mind that Beethoven did not see it in this way. There was, as he asserted to Ries, Czerny, and others, in each of his works a core of reality. This aspect of Beethoven much exercised Wagner, who wrote in this manner to Theodor Uhlig—'The characteristic mark of Beethoven's great compositions is that they are real poems; there is an attempt to represent a real object. . . . The essence of Beethoven's larger works is that the music in them is secondary; the main thing is the poetic object.' There were, however, difficulties in the way of comprehension for 'when the musical expression is conditioned by such an object the language becomes incomprehensible—unless indeed the object be indicated by some other means than music.'

According to this such music must be *de facto* 'programme music'. And this was the late Romantic conclusion. But Mendelssohn had something germane to say when he commented that music could be more definite than words, and its precision was beyond that of verbal logic. In short then each of Beethoven's symphonies has its origin in an idea from which music proceeds. Music outside the shape of the idea is eliminated. Thus artistic form emerges. 'Why do I write?' he asked himself. And his answer: 'What I have in my heart must come out; and that is why I compose.'

❡ EARLY SYMPHONIES · Of necessity a composer starts where others leave off. When the first symphony, in C major, was composed at the end of 1799 the great and beloved Viennese symphonist was Haydn, from whom Beethoven had had lessons some seven years previously. The mark of Haydn is clearly on the first and the second symphonies. So we may note the general shape of the first and last movements of each, the fuguing of the slow movement of the first, and the following *minuet*. More indefinable but no less evident is a common generosity of approach.

But there are other points to notice. The first symphony, *adagio molto* (in itself an index to deep feelings) commences out of key. C major is the advertised tonality. Imagine, then, the surprise of the Viennese audience when the first chord, attention drawn to it by the *pizzicato* strings, is palpably *not* in C major; not in C major, that is, as it was then pedantically understood. In fact by reference to the satellite tonalities of F and then of G Beethoven goes some way in making his principal key appear more prominent. After this initial shock the symphony aroused criticism on account of its scoring. There was, some said, too much woodwind and brass. In his first symphony Beethoven made these instruments full members of the orchestra. And in the slow movement the timpani stand out, thereby making the movement dramatic.

A wide range of keys and surprising transitions being part of his technique the music of Beethoven ranges far afield; as is shown in the introduction to the second symphony. This work of enchanting freshness is as it were an open-air piece, to be related by key and mood to the piano sonata in D major (Op. 10, No. 3). The first movement is enchantingly coloured throughout and (at bar 73) where clarinets, bassoons, and horns carry the first statement of the second principal melody, one is aware of a capacity for thinking a tune in instrumental terms. Here, says Tovey, is 'a certain almost military brilliance, which is in keeping with the fact that nobody wrote more formidably spirited marches than Beethoven'. Equally one may accept the tune as of popular provenance, symbolic of the composer's all-embracing intuition. The slow movement is in sonata form, with all its implications. That is to say it is continually unfolding new ideas which appear as the logical consequence of the opening motivs. This movement expresses deep, romantic, thought—the musical counterpart of Tieck or Novalis—punctuated by dramatic gestures, and illuminated by grace. In this connection consider the deportment of the strings. For the rest there is gaiety and humour in the scherzo and the finale, which is a magnificent example of blended rondo and sonata forms—by now the norm for last-movement structure. These formal developments, which were also in the later works of Haydn and Mozart, made for greater unity in the design; each movement being an entity with its sections closely welded.

There are commonplaces in Beethoven, for his thematic germs belong to the everyday speech of music. Notice especially his affection for scale passages, as at the beginning of the last movement of the first symphony or at the beginning of the introduc-

tion to the second. And when we turn to the third symphony—
the 'Eroica'—we discover that the prodigious first movement
starts its course with the same innocent arpeggio figure which
had played its part in probably a hundred eighteenth-century
pieces. Among them was the overture to Mozart's *Bastien and
Bastienne*.

❡ EROICA · It is, however, not the themes in themselves that
are important but the course that they direct. In the third symphony the vast scale of Beethoven's resourcefulness is fully
apparent. Here, too, one is aware of a new symphonic point of
view, for the subject is stated in the title. It is the hero, a concept
otherwise treated in the *Coriolanus* and *Egmont* overtures.

The heroic ideal—so focal a point in German Romantic philosophical and political speculation—is inescapable. In this symphony, as we read it, there is a fusion of ideals, raised to the level
of poetry by certain definitive observations, and then sublimated.
It is not without interest to compare this work with Schubert's
'Great C major' (heroic in all but name) and Schumann's tribute
to Beethoven himself in his magnificent *Phantasie*, also in C major;
and then with an 'heroic' work which is effective but palpably
limited—say Mendelssohn's *Reformation Symphony*. Schubert and
Schumann, under the shadow of Beethoven, understood the
function of music in this respect, whereas Mendelssohn did not.
After the 'revolutionary' hero-figure (for Beethoven picked up his
spacious if indeterminate general philosophy from the principles
fathered on the one hand by Rousseau and on the other by political exponents of Rousseau-ism) came the *Faust* hero (see Liszt,
Berlioz, Schumann), the *Don Juan* hero, the *Till Eulenspiegel* and
Don Quixote heroes (see Strauss) and the *Falstaff* hero (Elgar). So
we see how in Beethoven's music, which is almost entirely non-
realistic, the temper of his own age is reflected. Also we see how
in its own right it may be regarded as 'absolute'.

The *Sinfonia Eroica* gets down to business at once. The introduction is but two shattering chords of E flat. Then, quickly, the
opening theme is proposed by the cellos and continued until its
fuller character has been developed by lyrical and dramatic commentary. A peremptory six-note passage in octaves then heralds

a spacious sequence of second-group melodies. As is the custom with classical symphonies the exposition was to be repeated. In the development section as such (Beethoven's symphonies in effect are all development) there is reconsideration of previous material. But tonally we are on the edge of an unknown region: now in C major, now in C sharp minor, now in D minor, now in G minor, now in E minor.

In this remote key a quite new, lyrical episode arrives, in which the oboes and cellos in high register are prominent. The episode may be new but its coming is made to appear inevitable. It is repeated in E flat minor, and draws nearer to the fundamental tonal centre. The recapitulation is within sight when, at the end of the development, the shape of the first theme fills the ear with a sense of expectation, which is heightened by the mysteries hinted by the undercurrents of woodwind and strings.

Far away the violins alone tremble on the brink of silence. Across their dominant harmony comes a single horn—in tonic harmony—with the first four, fertile notes of the arpeggio theme. A classic and inexplicable place in musical theory. Why did Beethoven thus break the rules? The answer lies in the quotation on page 67. After the recapitulation is a lengthy peroration, or coda. The largest of classical first movements composed up to 1805, there is no doubting the heroic proportions.

In place of a slow movement is a *marcia funèbre*. Thus started another fashion (see Chopin's Sonata in B flat minor, Schumann's piano quintet and Elgar's second symphony). The funeral march is dominated by the immense first section, in itself an amalgam of passionate despair and certain hope. This is a commentary on general beliefs in last things, observing the pageantry of funeral ritual but not subordinate to it. The military bands play: but it is strings and not horns that tell us. The first episode is in C major (Beethoven used C minor and C major with similar associations of the tragic and the redemptive as did Handel) and the contrast of key is enhanced by the change wrought in the oboe, which had hitherto been plaintively conspicuous. The C major episode is irradiated by the subdued brilliance of string figuration and by the less funerary attire worn by the woodwind. (There is, in this

music, an invitation to those with the conviction that keys represent colours to state their case in favourable circumstances.) The
opening of the march comes again. Then a stern episode of which
the emotional character rises in part from the fugal method.
Finally a prodigious summary and expansion of the whole of the
funeral march proper. At the end there is a certainty that the
dominating impulse is of compassion.

But the symphony as a whole is concerned with life rather than
death. So the scherzo—all vivacity—supervenes. And after the
scherzo (the trio of which keeps the horns in hunting kit) the
finale, which is an invigorating set of variations. Apparently the
variations are on the theme given *pizzicato* after the brisk introductory bars. But this is illusion. The theme proper turns up in
the woodwind and is (perhaps) recognized as a *contre danse* from
the finale to the *Prometheus* music. The end of this movement is
in another fugue, based on first the bass motiv but later incor-
porating the *Prometheus* melody.

❬ SYMPHONY IV · The 'Eroica' was performed in 1805. It was
was succeeded by the symphony in B flat—Schumann's 'slender
Greek maiden between two Norse giants'. Yet, despite the general
ease of movement and playfulness of fancy, we should not be
misled. The slow introduction is Beethoven darkly contem-
plative, and the slow movement the quintessence of emotion
recollected in tranquillity. In this movement there is opportunity
to observe the dramatic—expressed in a pregnant rhythmic
formula—and the lyrical—the gracious tune made from a descending scale—in close collaboration. This, of course, is the hallmark
of Beethoven: his ability to see an idea in whole and not only
in part.

❬ UNKNOWN GODS · The fifth and sixth symphonies were first
performed, at the same concert, three days before Christmas in
1808. The programme also included the first performance of the
forward-looking *Choral Fantasia* (harbinger of the Choral Symphony), and the last performance of any concerto (the fourth) in
which Beethoven, his deafness now acute, was able to play the
solo part.

One need not go so far as to take the 'Destiny knocking at the

door' saying of Beethoven too literally; but it is hardly possible
to hear the fifth symphony and remain unaware that Fate, or
Destiny, was once a meaningful concept. Indeed, so it may be
still. Nor can one differ from Schumann when he wrote—'this
symphony invariably wields its power over men of every age like
those great pleasures of nature that fill us with fear and admiration at all times, no matter how frequently we may experience
them.'

Apart from the fact that the fifth symphony commences with
the most arresting figure in the whole of music (a fact which was
politically realized during the second world war) the work has
other compelling features. All of these equally reflect a vastness
of imagination, a comparable grasp of technical possibilities, and
restlessness with the established order. Deviations from the
accepted norm are perhaps fewer than one might expect, but
such as there are are sufficient to open the floodgates.

It is notably exposed, in fact, that Beethoven formed the pattern
of his music round his philosophic idea. The scherzo is an unquiet, unhappy episode in the symphony, and the fugal texture of
the trio gives small emotional relief. In the finale all appears to be
resolved. The mood is brilliant, the tunes impregnate with
optimism. Yet contrary thoughts may haunt the mind, and so—
midway through the movement—the scherzo makes unexpected
and sobering entry. Liszt found this departure 'interesting'.
Beethoven intended to stimulate more than interest—something
akin to the psalmist's 'in the midst of life . . .'.

There was once a small boy, Schumann tells us, who, on hearing the opening of the last movement, shivered and acknowledged
that he was frightened. The first impact of an enormous orchestra
can easily thus affect the newcomer. In this finale Beethoven un-
leashed what was for those days an incredible burst of sound, for
to the usual complement he had added piccolo, double bassoon
and three trombones.

In the slow movement two points stand out: the warm ecstasy
of the opening theme which derives half of its quality from the
colour of violas and cellos, and the glorious subsequent outburst
in C major. Although the movement as a whole is in the key of

A flat major (an unexpected choice of key) that of C major, being the tonic major of the whole symphony, brings it into tonal relation with its surroundings.

In his greatest movements the principal themes in themselves are guides to the imaginative limits of the music. Note especially how this is the case in the first movement of the fifth symphony, where an enormous stretch of imagination lies between the initial motiv and the affectionate temper of the second subject, which lies in the key of E flat major. This theme is heralded by the horns engaged in the all-pervasive four-note figure. Later, in the recapitulation, Beethoven's horns could not undertake this duty. Not being valve horns, and without time to change their crooks so as to move from E flat to C major, they were impotent. Thus the bassoon stands in for them. Should we, or should we not, now ascribe to the horns what is, but was not, within their competence? Probably we should. In this instance the composer acted as he did against inclination.

The sixth symphony, which was written before the fifth, is no less serious than its neighbours. For Beethoven, as every Romantic artist, was very serious indeed about Nature, and there was a good deal of reading in 'Nature's mystic book'.

The outstanding movement of the five which constitute the *Pastoral Symphony* is the second. This is at once a marvellously contrived sonata-form movement, with rather more in the way of thematic variety than was generally the case, a landscape painting, and a philosophic commentary. The movement is entitled 'By the brook side'. If the rhythm, the liquidity of the melodies, the originality of the evocative scoring, suggest the movement of water all very well and good. If not it hardly matters. About the symphony as a whole Beethoven said that it was 'the expression of feelings rather than painting'. Thus it is the contentment, the freedom from tension that may be enjoyed by a stream on a summer's day that is defined: not the stream.

In this symphony, however, the composer could not entirely escape the itch to delineate. The first movement ('Awakening of happy feelings on getting out into the country') is filled with people, in that the tunes are patently of rustic origin; so too is

the scherzo—the 'merry gathering of the country folk'. These
two movements, slyly humorous, are light of foot and credit the
Viennese peasantry with qualities of wit brighter than they may
be supposed to have displayed. But at that time every rural settle-
ment was in the province of Arcadia, and idealization is one of
the functions of music. Malignancy lay with the unseen, un-
knowable faces, to whose secret presence Beethoven draws attention in the catastrophic thunderstorm movement, which prefaces
the final 'Shepherd's Song: Happy and thankful feelings after
the storm'.

The *Pastoral Symphony*, then, is explicitly an expression of feeling. Whose feeling? In the first place Beethoven's. In the second
yours and mine. The test is to put oneself into similar environment. But our feelings are, generally, less productive. Therefore
we are grateful to Beethoven for acting on our behalf. Behind
one's own insubstantial recollections of mood lie the evidences
of the day: the 'oaten stop, or pastoral song', the beetle winding
'his small but sullen horn'. The background 'realities' of Beethoven's symphony are justified by experience.

❡ A MATTER OF RHYTHM · There is an exciting passage in
Holst's *Hymn of Jesus*: 'divine grace is dancing'. And divine grace
catches us all up sooner or later into the spiritual ecstasy. Something of this symbolism lies behind the seventh symphony; which
is what was meant by Wagner in his famous summary of the
work as the 'apotheosis of the dance'.

There are two circumstances which may or may not have anything to do with the actual music, but which affected Beethoven's
sympathies at the time of composition.

The war against Napoleon was at its crisis. In 1812 Napoleon
was defeated in Russia and in Spain; and Austria joined with
Russia, Prussia, and Sweden to fight the campaign in Germany
which led to the victorious climax, in 1813, at Leipzig. On the
one hand military victory; on the other (as the parents of Wagner
and Schumann knew) great suffering. The seventh symphony
was composed in 1812 and first performed (with the *Battle
Symphony*) in December 1813, at a concert organized by Johann
Maelzel in aid of soldiers wounded at the Battle of Hanau.

But while he was considering the seventh symphony Beethoven was also engaged in a commission (from George Thomson of Edinburgh) to arrange a set of Irish folk-songs. The theme of the finale of the symphony is said to bear some resemblance to one of these folk-songs.

The introduction to the first movement is a vast ante-chamber to the whole structure—a movement in itself, based on an ever-expanding scale motiv (prefaced by an oboe melody) on the one hand, and a march theme aptly commanded by the woodwind on the other. Between introduction and first movement is one note—the dominant—many times repeated, now by woodwind now by strings. Then flutes and oboes, soon joined by bassoons, clarinets, and horns, deliver the gay 6/8 dance rhythm which pervades the whole of the movement. The vitality of the first movement is balanced by the exuberance of the last. Rarely does a composer achieve such symmetry when dealing with such different musical material. The complementary character of the outside movements is enhanced by the contrast of the middle movements.

The second movement, of which the opening wind chord of A minor is by no means the least impressive feature, is a march—another funeral march. (Romain Rolland describes it as 'elegiac' and 'pageant-like.') The rhythm is stern, the colouring—with violas at the top of the score—grave. In the first movement the manner in which the music expanded was impressive. So also is it here. Against the initial melody there soon sounds a counter-subject—such contrapuntal evolution inevitably increases the range; but, gradually, all the instrumental forces are moved until (at bar 75) melody and counter-melody blaze forth in sombre magnificence. A change from A minor to A major, where clarinet and bassoon sing against the ripple of triplets in the violins recalls the first consolatory episode in the 'Eroica'. Beneath this passage, however, the rhythm of the march still treads. There is further affinity with the 'Eroica' when the repetition of the first section leads into fugal devolution. The end of the *allegretto* (which Beethoven later thought he should have marked *andante*) is another illustration of the way in which the composer conceived instrumental tone-colour as an integral part of musical thought.

For the *scherzo* Beethoven chose the key of F major—left over as it were from the *Pastoral Symphony*. But the speed—*presto*—removes us from rural jollity: there is fire in the music. If the flames rise high in the *presto* then the trio, in D major and with horns prominent in the wind band which takes charge, glows incandescently. Both *scherzo* and *trio* are repeated and the movement ends with a coda in which the elements of both are again reconsidered.

¶ SCHERZANDO · Sometimes the directions at the head of movements tell us all we need to know of the 'meaning' of music. In respect of the eighth symphony this is certainly the case. *Allegro vivace e con brio*: the first movement in carefree three time has all that is signified therein. As in the seventh symphony (Beethoven was at work on both in the same year, 1812) there is no slow movement. Here again is an *allegretto*, but this term is qualified by another—*scherzando*. 'Skittish' is the near-enough translation.

Johann Maelzel has previously been mentioned in connection with the performance of the seventh symphony. He, at this time a friend of Beethoven, was also an inventor, responsible for the 'Maelzel' metronome. His scientific qualities called from Beethoven a catch, in which the rhythmic basis was the tick of the Stockel-Maelzel 'chronometer'. It was this catch which served as the starting-point of the second movement of the eighth symphony: hence the appositeness of *scherzando*. Something of the *scherzando* mood may be found to have communicated itself also to the first movement—in the early solo behaviour of the bassoon, in the interchanging positions of the woodwind instruments generally, in the silent and pause bars which hold the listener momentarily intrigued, and in the *papillon* flutter in the last two bars.

But this is a symphony and not a sinfonietta (even though Beethoven affectionately termed it his 'little one'), and the last movement is large and comprehensive. Compare the first subject with the second, which appears in the first violins at bar 48. The key now is not F major, but A flat major. One of the fascinating qualities of this finale is the manner in which distant keys are used for their romantic effect although they are contained within a unified tonal framework. All is controlled by a certain logic. Thus the prominent C sharp, which lies at the end of the first subject and is emphasized by the *ff* breaking in on *ppp*, relates to the totally unexpected use of F sharp minor tonality towards the end of the movement.

'I always have the whole in my mind.' So Beethoven wrote of his method of composition to Georg Treitschtze. We have seen the *scherzando* idea in the first two movements. It is even more intensified in the finale; but there are still elements of simple comedy about. So once again we turn to the bassoon—the court jester of the classical orchestra—and notice how it joins the timpani in anticipating the recapitulation. At this point also we are aware of a difference in the drums. Formerly they were tuned in fifths. Here they are tuned an octave apart.

The eighth symphony is Haydnesque in that it covers some of the territory formerly occupied by Haydn. But music can never say the same thing twice. And the minuet which Beethoven substitutes for his more usual *scherzo* is no eighteenth-century minuet. At first it may sound like it, but the urgency of trumpets and horns, the authoritative romantic flavour of clarinet and horns in the trio, are of the nineteenth century. The reversion to minuet is of course, purposeful. The operative word is contrast, and a *scherzo* amid *scherzando* would represent no contrast.

Beethoven's contemporaries did not much like the eighth symphony. It was too small (thus we notice 'bigness' as an end in itself—a facet of popular thought still with us). On occasion, therefore, it was dignified by the substitution of the second movement by the *allegretto* from the seventh symphony. A tribute, of sorts, to that movement, whose popularity was immense. Why the eighth symphony was ill received, and why it still receives fewer performances than it should, lies in the word 'significance'. In comparison with the larger symphonies the eighth appeared insignificant; that is, it appeared to communicate ideas that in themselves were of small consequence. Beethoven himself was partly responsible for the growth of portentousness (hence the kind of reverent utterance issued by Pauer and quoted at the beginning of this book); but his own philosophy did not ignore small things.

¶ CHORAL SYMPHONY · Ten years separated the seventh and eighth from the ninth symphony, which was performed—together with some parts of the *Missa Solennis*—on 7 May 1824. In all the late works there is an intensity of expression and of feeling that defies immediate comprehension. Here music approaches as near as it can to philosophy. The words of J. W. N. Sullivan are relevant:

'Beethoven's late music communicates experiences that very few people can normally possess. But we value these experiences because we feel they are not freakish. They correspond to a spiritual synthesis which the race has not achieved but which, we may suppose, is on the way to achieving. It is only the very greatest kind of artist who presents us with experiences that we recognize both as fundamental and as in advance of anything we have hitherto known.'

Hitherto the term 'musical appreciation' may have had some significance in the symphonic pilgrimage. To apply it in any way to the Ninth would merely mislead. This is music which we 'know' or do not 'know'. Experience helps; but experience of synthesis rather than of analysis. At once it might be said that one should try to become acclimatized to Beethoven's last-period music as a whole. For by listening to the 'Hammerclavier' sonata, the *Missa Solennis*, the A minor quartet (Op. 132) and the *Grosse Fuge*, one comes to recognize a musico-philosophic purpose. And in all these works the qualities which we have learned to recognize as of Beethoven emerge in idealized character, and none independent of other.

A composer carries the idea of a great work with him through most of his working life. He may, or may not, achieve his objective. In the case of Beethoven—even though a tenth symphony was projected—we feel that he did. In the ninth symphony Beethoven combined the plans for two separate works: the one set for a great symphony, the other for an ample expression of Schiller's 'Ode to Joy'. Sketches for the latter were in existence when the symphony was undertaken. And at first the final symphonic movement was to be purely instrumental. But the material for this movement was translated to the finale of the A minor quartet —an additional reason for listening to that work.

And here it must be said that Beethoven miscalculated. The choral finale is less effective than the previous movements. Partly because Beethoven's interest in the choral medium was relatively slight, partly because the musical ideas are commonplace, if not, indeed banal. It is as though, after the objectivity of the first three movements, Beethoven has remembered his personal involvements and has put on a cloak of optimism. Bass drum, triangle, cymbals come into the scheme of things, inevitably to bring the music somewhat nearer the fairground than one might expect. But all this happens after more than forty minutes of sublime music have passed. Whirlwinds and storms are part of the imagery of poetical interpretation. For reasons which have been expounded Beethoven was conscious of such phenomena, and to admit their significance was part of the responsibility—as he saw it—to his generation. It would be pardonable for the listener whose understanding is quickened by the transference of musical effect to visual concept if he were to relate the rhythms and layout of the first two movements and the widely contrasted 'deep dream of peace' of the *adagio molto* to the vocabulary of nature. But this is insufficient: for the music is of one who rides on the whirlwind, and directs the storm. In short the vision and the material of expression is controlled by supreme intellectual power. In more ways than one the ninth symphony is the summary of the greatness of the aspiration of Romantic thought:

> *. . . the unimaginable lodge*
> *For solitary thinkings; such as dodge*
> *Conception to the very bourne of heaven,*
> *Then leave the naked brain.*

There is a way towards the heart of Beethoven's music by way of Keats's *Endymion*.

In the fifth and seventh symphonies especially there was something fundamental about the cogent motivs. So, too, here, though

one might prefer 'elemental' to 'fundamental'. What is the first
movement about? At once, and obviously, the interval of the
fifth, and from the sixteenth bar the sounds which constitute the
minor chord. There is a lot more to it than this, for the argument
of the movement is far-reaching; but the primal origins are never
out of sight. The nature of the thematic and, especially, rhythmic
material, together with their working-out, makes the music comprehensive. We are at the beginning of things, and also at the
end. And the scherzo, which in this symphony comes second,
likewise springs from the background of emotion and music.
The predominating octave leaps (note how, as in the previous
symphony, the drums are tuned in octaves), the urgent rhythm is
the exemplification of John Donne's 'Batter my heart, three-
person'd God.' An enormous movement—relieved by the trio in
major tonality which, however, in itself is something of a technical *tour de force*—the scherzo crosses the common pattern with
that of sonata. Thus it is seen how from being a recreational
interlude the third symphonic movement has now achieved a
stature of its own.

The intellectual urgency does not slacken. The slow movement (in the key of B flat) consists of two themes (the second,
beginning at bar 25, in D major and thus keeping its sights
trained on the ultimate tonal objective). And this development is
in variation form. Though here, truly, it might be said that the
term 'symphonic variations' applies. In the slow movement of
the second symphony Beethoven was on the way towards the
sublime. How much further he was to travel is shown by the
index of his solitary, voyaging mind. It is sufficient to notice
what happens in the course of the movement to the opening
fragment of violin melody—two descending fourths: again
elemental.

One could, perhaps, leave the ninth symphony at this point.
But Beethoven, not lacking in the didactic impulse that was part
of Romanticism, needed both to complete the traditional scheme
with a fourth movement and also to humanize his philosophy.
So the final cantata-theme-with-variations, in which is the vision
of a brave new world.

VI. Beethoven's Predecessors

❡ WILLIAM BOYCE (1710–1779) · The indelible impression left
by the symphonic works of Beethoven is their 'high seriousness'
—as Matthew Arnold would have termed it. To turn back, however, to the works of other composers in the same field of twenty-
five years earlier is to recognize a different intention. Flippancy is
perhaps derogatory; but J. C. Bach, Abel, Sammartini, Martini,
and company, would have scorned the notion that symphonies
existed for the purpose of 'uplift'.

C. P. E. Bach, indeed, said as much. For 'learned music' he had
no time. Counterpoint was not the main end of composition.
Canons were 'dry and despicable pieces of pedantry that anyone
might compose who would give his time to them'. In all of which
was more than a grain of truth; and the 'learned' composers of
today might sometimes consider the point.

As it happens the earliest available recorded symphonies give
a clue to the type of music which the *avant garde* composers of
the mid-eighteenth century wished to displace.

Culled from various sources (New Year Odes, music for plays, for the Three Choirs Festival—which he conducted) the symphonies of William Boyce are similar in form to *concerti grossi*. Thus their first movements have a massive quality which grows from vigorous bass parts. In his slow movements, however, Boyce showed that stolidity was not his sole virtue. The aria movement of the first symphony, for example, has a sinuous line of melody guided by those gently distracting harmonies that distinguished the contemporary Italian school, and were to be developed so significantly by Mozart. In his 6/8 finales—sophisticated jigs—Boyce would appear to stand mid-way between Handel and Haydn.

Nevertheless, even when alluringly arranged by Constant Lambert for the ballet *The Prospect Before Us*, one is always aware of the conservative disposition; not for the last time in English music. Correctness of form, clarity of design, and a respect for the inclinations of his sober public are all evident; but, with a distinctive melodic gift, they make pleasurable listening, and even more pleasurable playing.

❡ THOMAS AUGUSTINE ARNE (1710–1778) · If Boyce worthily represented the central tradition of English music Thomas Augustine Arne stood for a more adventurous strain. Eminently a man of the theatre Arne had greater awareness of the changing temper of taste. In the best sense Boyce was insular. Arne endeavoured not so to be. Thus, in 1762, he wrote his Italianate opera *Artaserse*. Of this the overture shows the essential characteristics of the *galant* style—and its derivation from *opera buffa*. The first movement contains all the light-weight clichés neatly assorted in the new symphonic manner, and scored with effective delicacy. If in the two succeeding movements Arne moves back a pace or two it makes no odds. The first movement stands as the sign of the times.

❡ JOHN CHRISTIAN BACH (1735–1782) AND CARL FRIEDRICH ABEL (1725–1787) · It was in 1762 that John Christian Bach came to England, to compose for the theatre. Two years later he collaborated with Carl Friedrich Abel—one of the last of J. S. Bach's pupils—in concert promotion. This venture pursued a successful course for seventeen years. Concerts—notable features of London social life—were given at Spring Gardens, at the concert rooms of Almack's and Hanover Square, at private houses (see a reference to Mrs Cornelys's Assembly in Smollett's *Humphry Clinker*). And the mainstay of the programmes was symphonies: Italian-style symphonies—for J. C. Bach had lived for five impressionable years in Milan—of which a number were by Abel and by Bach himself. Those by Abel are of rather less interest than those by Bach, for the latter wrote with a verve and brilliance that was foreign to Abel.

In 1764 Mozart visited London. He was received with great kindness by Abel and Bach, and was deeply impressed by the quality of their works. So much so that he copied works by both, which now have their place in the Mozart canon: (Symphony No. 3, K.18, in E flat was transcribed from Abel, while the three piano concertos of K.107 were transcriptions of sonatas by J. C. Bach).

The extraordinary influence of the Italian *sinfonia* is illustrated in the works of at least three of the younger Bachs: Carl Philipp Emanuel, Johann Christoph Friedrich, and John Christian. In the works of the two former there is more of originality and more of experiment than in those of the latter. The direction is towards the mature Haydn. In John Christian, on the other hand, whose output was very large, there is a complete catalogue of the qualities of *galant* art. The implications of *galant* and the restrictions of the style recall mediaeval parallels in the formal exercises of troubadour and trouvère.

Highly professional music, J. C. Bach's symphonies are elegantly contrived, with no great emotional impact, and deliciously scored. With his little band of strings, oboes, and horns, with harpsichord, he gives the impression of knowing exactly what disposition of timbres is most effective. Within the narrow limits the symphonies of Op. 9 and Op. 18 are a delight to the ear. But Bach had an eye for wider horizons. Consider the *sinfonia* for double orchestra (Op. 18 No. 1) in which one band of oboes, bassoon, and strings contrasts with a smaller body of flutes and strings, or the various *sinfonii concertanti*. In such works one is reminded of the partial descent of symphony from the older concerto.

In fact J. C. Bach wrote more symphonies (forty-nine, as well as thirty-one *sinfonii concertanti*) than Mozart. But one would be hard put to it to suggest at what period of his life particular works were written. In Mozart one can, and because of this one can see a development of style and purpose that was beyond the capacity of the youngest and most agreeable of the sons of J. S. Bach.

❡ WOLFGANG AMADEUS MOZART (1756–1791) · Of all the great musicians Mozart is at once the most and the least comprehensible. As has been seen the purpose of much music can be understood by analogy. Sometimes—as in the cases of Bach and Beethoven—a philosophic pattern can be traced. Sometimes, as in respect of Schumann, or Liszt, or Strauss, such literary connections as may stimulate are often rewarding appreciation of aspects of poetry or drama. Or there is an endemic parochialism ready to respond generously to nationalistic fervour—which often comes out in music as little more than parish-pride. Mozart obliges in none of these particulars. His symphonies are removed from any philosophizing (except what writers invent and ascribe to him), from any literary associations, from any aspect of nationalism. They are, indeed, abstract; in the basic meaning just symphonies.

It is, perhaps, safe to say that Mozart was the most purely *musical* of composers, and the most professional. Of his life it is not necessary to say much here. But his prowess as a child; the completely inexplicable creative talent with which he arrived in the world; the pride, persistence, and opportunism of his father (who saw in the greater genius of his son his own fulfilment) should be recalled in considering why his career was as it was. Music was inescapable. Mozart could only pursue the one course. This being so he must needs attempt to adjust himself to society.

A musician in eighteenth-century Austria (as Maria Theresa remarked on more than one occasion) was expected to accept servility. Most did; but not Mozart. No inferiority complex assailed him; but intellectual equality could be demonstrated only in one way—by writing music. As we see it, then, Mozart accepted the obligation laid upon him to compose and, aware of the social function of music in the age in which he lived, obeyed certain conventions. But his inner convictions regarding his essential significance inflamed him so that an inflexible will is the true mark of Mozart. It is that which distinguishes his music.

Thus we may remove the too feminine approach which has affected both the performance and the appreciation of Mozart. Grace, gentle melancholy, wit, fine proportions are all to be discerned; but they are incidental. The notable symphonies of Mozart are so because they represent music in its purity. That being so it is to each to read into them what he will.

In 1843 the French musician Michel Bourgès commented on the 'elegance and charm of detail' of the 'Jupiter' symphony, whereas the Russian Alexander Oulibichev observed that it might have been 'commanded and written to celebrate some mighty event in the world's history'. The symphony in G minor (K.550) was described by Berlioz as a 'model of delicacy and naïveté', but by Nissen, who married Mozart's widow, as 'the expression of a restless and uneasy passion'. About such comment there is neither right nor wrong; which only goes to show the universality of the music. And this it was that stirred Leigh Hunt:

> *and Mozart universal,*
> *But chiefly with exquisite gallantries found,*
> *With a grove, in the distance, of holier sound.*

At the present time we are divided into those who find a prophylactic influence in the 'holier sound', those who nostalgically collect the 'gallantries', because such graces have long departed both from life and from music, and those who perceive a clarity in Mozartian execution that matches the precise beauty of some parts of contemporary mathematical and scientific thought. The true Mozart-philes, I am told, are at Harwell or Calder Hall.

It is clear from the music itself that Mozart was a perfectionist. But such a degree of perfection as was achieved came from constant application.

EARLY ESSAYS · At first the boy Mozart happily followed the manner of J.C.Bach, as may be seen in those charming symphonic exercises of 1765 and 1766, with their self-consciously formal first movements, graceful *andantes*, and gay rondos in 3/8 time. In these works the influence of the Italian *sinfonia* is strong, and certain aspects of this influence remained. So that rhythmic precision, elegance in melodic contour, clarity of texture were never obscured by later developments.

It was impossible, however, to be home in Salzburg and unaware of the music being composed in Vienna, and knowledge of the works of Wagenseil and Haydn led to a more expansive idea of symphony. In the symphony in F (K.43) the violas are divided, according to a Viennese convention, the wind parts are fuller, and a minuet is set between the *andante* and finale. The close proximity of symphony to opera—otherwise shown at this time by the use of the symphony in D (K.45) as an overture to *La finta semplice*—is exemplified in this *andante*, which is a transcription of a song from a comedy-piece—*Apollo et Hyacinthus*—written for a group of university students.

In these early symphonies the formal design appears now, not unnaturally, as rather too stylized. First movement form shows two subjects, the first generally square and made from an arpeggio figure and the second more fluid, more melodious. The exposition ended, the next section starts with the first subject in the key of the dominant, as in many keyboard pieces of the preceding generation. After repetitive material the second subject returns in the key of the tonic. So, in effect, the essential tripartite plan has not yet emerged.

In the symphony in D (K.48), which was composed at the end of his long stay in Vienna in 1768, Mozart shows a great advance. The opening of the symphony is arresting in the unexpected leaps in the first violin part. There is a development section—in which chords fall unexpectedly (see bar 4 of this section), and in which horns and trumpets and oboes assert their independence—and a full recapitulation. The slow movement is now not embroidered in the graceful Italian way, but simple and serious and subject to interruption by dramatic gestures. Expression, as shown in dynamic markings, is now important, and this being so we come within sight of the Romantic revolution.

IN ITALY · Between 1770 and 1772 Mozart was a good deal in

Italy, where he was impressed especially by the music of Sammartini and influenced by the teaching of Martini. It was Sammartini who was partly responsible for the development of fluency in Mozart's writing and Martini who introduced him to the excitements of contrapuntal development within symphonic form. In this period Mozart composed sixteen symphonies (some obedient to the Italian manner to the extent of dispensing with the minuet), which are marked by an added certainty in design, by a fluent instrumental facility, by a technique that in itself was accomplished beyond anything then known.

What others did, he normally did better.

In these teen-age works Mozart begins to show how, having mastered the elements of style and expression, he can accommodate himself to the general and also carry his symphonic ideas to an imaginative plane. In the first movement of K.114 the second subject group (bar 36 *et seq*) is an impressive blend of diverse propositions, and the *andante* an ethereal piece with just sufficient chromatic inflexions to point towards the *Ave Verum* of 1791, while in the third movement there is intensity beyond the intention of a commonplace dance in the imitative entries and tonal contrast of the trio—a bitter-sweet interlude. The symphonies in C and E flat (which keys thread significantly into the general sequence of Mozart's works)—K.128 and K.132, show two cardinal points of Mozart's musical personality; the former in its controlled celerity, the latter in rich tonal contrasts and original disposition of sonorities. It is, however, the symphony in D (K.133) which may be seen as an essential link between the works of childhood and maturity.

This work is full both of grace and of power; it is at once innocent and wise. A festive first movement, brilliantly lit by trumpets and horns, is fertile in melodic invention. The scintillating figuration of the strings is distinctively Italian, but something is reflected of the gravity of an older style—that of Durante and Jommelli. And this grave element is heightened by the four-note chromatic motiv derived from the exposition—which runs through the development like a *cantus firmus*. A few years later Mozart would have done even more with this sort of figure, as in the last movement of the 'Jupiter' symphony; but as it is one can only marvel at the superb architecture of a splendid conception.

The mastery of instrumental resource which marks this symphony is shown in its most gracious form in the slow movement: a piece which still carries the impress of J. C. Bach but which is so certain of itself that it can carry one seemingly trivial triplet figure through almost all of its 102 bars without becoming wearisome. Indeed one of the remarkable features of Mozart is his capacity for transmuting the commonplace figures that were also to be encountered in the most trivial works of other composers. And all that is used is the string ensemble and a solo flute. But by now the strings are fully exploited; a token of which is the viola end-piece to the magical ending of the exposition. The earnest quality of the minuet, the vivid scoring for wind, especially in the last movement, a general robust undertone, a care for nuance, again suggest the influence of Haydn.

INDEPENDENCE OF SYMPHONY · Symphony, despite its occasional origins, is, by now, beginning to establish its own independent life. It is noticeable how the growing individuality of Mozart's symphonies is associated with his growing dramatic power as shown at this time in *Lucio Silla*. By far the most dramatic symphony among Mozart's earlier examples is that in G minor (K.183); the first of his symphonies to be cast in a minor key. In the restlessness, both rhythmic and harmonic, of the first few bars is the first shape of the greater G minor symphony of 1788. More patently perhaps than in any other symphony of this time K.183 shows a unity of intention: the dominant impulse of passion is equally evident in the first, third, and last movements.

This symphony in G minor serves to emphasize the range of Mozart's vision. Compare it, for example, with the tolerably familiar outlines of the A major symphony of 1774 (K.201), or the authority of the pellucid work in C major (K.200), in both of which de Saint-Foix sees the sober influence of Mozart's Salzburg companion Michael Haydn, brother of Josef.

Such variety as has already been disclosed as the work of a boy still in his eighteenth year can be explained quite simply as the fruit of imagination. But there is another point. Mozart was the most adaptable of workmen. He could adapt himself to Milan, Vienna, Salzburg, Paris, or Prague, presenting his thoughts with an awareness of the local idiom. He wrote church music, opera, symphony, serenade with equal fertility. He learned to interpret the rites of freemasonry on the one hand and the good fortune of the Haffners on the other.

MIDDLE PERIOD WORKS · Between 1774 and 1778 there was a gap in Mozart's symphonic output. But the work which he produced for the *Concerts Spirituels* in Paris (K.297) is important as showing another stage in development. This work is scored for a large orchestra with such instruments as were not available in Salzburg but whose properties Mozart had come to recognize at Mannheim, where he was in 1777. The 'Paris' symphony for the first time in Mozart's symphonies shows the complete classical ensemble of double woodwind, horns, trumpets, drums, and strings.

Careful to acclimatize himself to Parisian taste Mozart commenced this symphony with an eruptive four bars by the full orchestra (in which, for once, the internal disposition of the harmony is hardly satisfactorily balanced): the *premier coup d'archet*, which was a Parisian convention. About this Mozart was cynical: 'I have hopes that the asses too may see something in it to delight them.' And one suspects that a contempt for his French patrons—increased by the unhappy fate of the *sinfonia concertante* he had previously written but failed to get performed, and his inability substantially to improve his prospects—was the reason for this symphony wearing a casual expression.

Of the familiar symphonies the 'Paris' is in fact the least Mozartian. But as this is the general opinion attention might be drawn to the last bars of the development of the first movement, where, with a characteristic sleight of hand, the music is switched into the key of F major; and to the nimble counterpoint of the finale.

After writing his symphony in Paris Mozart returned to Salzburg with what he had learned of French music fresh in his mind. The result was the one-movement symphony in G (K.318), with a normal first-movement form interrupted at the end of the exposition by a gentle *andante*, after which follows a telescoped development and recapitulation. This in effect is a symphonic overture, patterned after Gossec or other French composers and the model for the overture to *Die Entführung aus dem Serail*.

The companion piece to K.318 is K.319, in B flat, a work that is both witty and whimsical. In the rhythmic flavouring of the first movement may be detected a characteristically Viennese quality such as later shows in the symphonies of Schubert. For this symphony the orchestra is small—oboes, bassoons and horns and strings—according to the available players in Salzburg. The minuet which now belongs was an addition to the original plan, made for performance in Vienna. A third symphony for Salzburg, in the dispiriting years 1779–80, was that in C major (K.338), of which the features are the romantic aspirations (see the end of the development section) within the ceremonial brilliance of the first movement, the serenity of the *andante* for strings, and the fierce *saltarello* energy of the 6/8 finale.

IN VIENNA · It was shortly after the completion of these commissions that Mozart left the service of the Archbishop of Salzburg and settled permanently in Vienna. Much else happened in the two years which preceded the composition of the next symphony. *Idomeneo* was produced in Munich, *Die Entführung* was composed, and personal affairs reached a climax when Mozart became engaged to Constanze Weber against his father's wishes. But maturity in more ways than one was reached. So, rightly, the 'Haffner' symphony, K.385, of July 1782, is regarded as the first of the great symphonies of the final phase. The Haffner family, of Salzburg, for whom Mozart had composed one serenade (K.250) in 1776—a work which anticipates *Don Giovanni* in respect of certain rhythmic formulae—hastily called for a second. The reason was the ennoblement of Siegmund Haffner.

Austrian serenades had hitherto borne an easy prolixity: music against which conversation might be sustained and refreshments served. (The nearest thing we understand to this aspect of eighteenth-century music are the strains supplied by long-suffering members of the Musicians' Union at the Mayor's inaugural reception. Remember that Mozart earned a large part of his livelihood in that manner.) The 'Haffner' symphony in its serenade form had an introductory march, and a second minuet, and was without flutes and clarinets. But what is now the first movement of the symphony must have been shattering. Nothing of the facile gallantry, the conventional *desipere in loco*, the ear-tickling tunefulness that might have been expected; but a cutting brilliance, an irresistible energy which the insistent first theme and the fugal writing convey with chiselled precision. Living in Vienna and associating with Baron van Swieten, whose enthusiasm for Bach and Handel was considerable, Mozart had come to a deeper understanding of the contrapuntal aspect of music. The 'Haffner' symphony shows its complete absorption into the already distinctive Mozart idiom. The last movement of the 'Haffner' symphony is, of course, a foreshadowing of the overture to *Figaro*

In the 'Linz' symphony (K.425) there is evidence of much reading of Handel in the vigorous thrusts of plain tonic and sub-dominant harmony which produce unmistakable Alleluias. But there is also much of Haydn in the plan of the symphony. Particularly notable in this respect are the slow introduction (a less frequent feature in Mozart than in Haydn), the poetic quality of the *poco adagio*, and the rhythm of the finale. But Mozart's acceptance of Haydn's alterations in the character of symphony did not affect his belief in his own powers. Thus it is that there is no bar in the work which is not patently Mozartian. We are brought again to the extraordinary blend of grace and power: *suaviter in modo, fortiter in re*. Consider the authority of the slow movement wherein the trumpets and horns are surprisingly retained, and the sylph-like movement of the minuet—the purest ballet.

The symphony in D (K.504), lies between *Figaro* and *Don Giovanni* in point of time, and is to be seen in relation to those two works as a kind of essay on certain of their aspects. The slow introduction is charged with the gravity of the more philosophical passages in *Don Giovanni*, and the slow movement with the atmosphere of Count Almaviva's garden at midnight. This symphony was written prior to visiting Prague at the beginning of 1787. But clearly Mozart had the Bohemians in mind when he was writing. The animation of the first movement, the brilliance and variety of the scoring alone were sufficient to ensure its welcome. And so it proved. The 'Prague' symphony was an instant success.

CLIMAX · Throughout his career Mozart had been seconding Haydn in the emancipation of symphonic style. Haydn was the formalist—in that he settled the general pattern which symphonic composers have accepted for two centuries—and the pioneer in emotional enlargement. Mozart gave to symphony a comprehensive character. It has been noted how almost every other aspect of his music has been reflected in this symphony or that; how impressions received from many places and people have been worked into the pattern. In these symphonies—the great trilogy of 1788—Mozart shows symphonic music at a climax.

In the symphonies in E flat (K.543), G minor (K.550), and C major (K.551), the classical ideal is attained. All the elements that previously were separately discernible are entirely interfused. These works are not redolent of particular aspects of eighteenth-century behaviour, nor relevant to operatic situations, nor divisible into spheres of influence. They are unified creations existing solely in their own right.

Unity in art is often misunderstood, being too much entangled with the matter of form. Balance and proportion will ensure a kind of unity, and by attention to the precepts anyone, within reason, may produce an elementary consistency. But the essential unity is of idea. Its presence it truly felt only when it can be sensed that a poem, or a play, or a sculpture, or a musical work, has existed as a whole before its composition has been effected. Beethoven claimed that this was the case in respect of his works. It is to be believed. And so it assuredly is in the case of Mozart's last three symphonies.

When, within the space of seven weeks in the summer of 1788, he was engaged on their writing out, Mozart, by all normal laws, should have been incapable of such a feat. In debt, disillusioned, discouraged, the pitiable state into which he had sunk is illustrated by his letters to Michael Puckberg. 'Owing to great difficulties and complications', he wrote at the beginning of July, after completing the symphony in E flat, 'my affairs have become so involved that it is of the utmost importance to raise some money on these two pawnbroker's tickets. In the name of our friendship I implore you to do me this favour; but you must do it immediately.'

How, under such conditions, does a creative artist work? Look back at p. 65 and see again how pertinent is Thomas Mann's generalization. The fact is that the music was there—the embedded pearl. The setting of it down to one with Mozart's experience and facility was almost automatic. Almost—but not quite. The coda to the slow movement of the 'Jupiter' symphony was an afterthought. While the scoring of the G minor symphony was revised to admit clarinets.

A hundred years ago Wagner complained of the indifferent performances of Mozart then common. 'Mozart', he wrote 'who was intimately acquainted with the noble style of Italian singing, whose musical expression derived its very soul from the delicate vibrations, swellings and accents of that style, was the first to reproduce the effects of this vocal style, by means of orchestral instruments.' And it was in the E flat symphony that he found this quality at its height. This, then, may be taken as the full expression of Mozart's lyrical genius. The G minor symphony, on the other hand, is tragically cast. In each case notice how all the movements of each symphony are conducive to one end. The test movement is always the minuet. Mozart was hitherto never quite certain whether this dance merited its place in the symphonic scheme: these two minuets prove how essential it was in the final phase.

Literary criticism has always been torn between two dogmas; expressed respectively as 'holding up a mirror to nature', and 'criticism of life'. Within limits the G minor and E flat symphony hold up the mirror, whereas the 'Jupiter' is the more critical. Or, if not critical, then more detached. If one wishes one can read Mozart's 1788 frame of mind into the music of the first two; but not in any way into the last of the trilogy. This, it is suggested, is how life should be; not as it is. So the last movement is a masterly essay in counterpoint, in the working out of relationships between five separate themes—none greatly memorable except in their context. And the crowning theme—that of four notes—has, as it were, a higher authority. It is to be found far back in the tradition of plainsong—and it may well have come to Mozart, for it was a frequent theme for academic exercise, by way of Padre Martini.

A symphony is comprehensive. Turn back to the first movement, to the second subject. Here is a transliteration of a comic aria (issued independently as K.541). And then to the supreme beauty of the slow movement in which the poignancy of the modulations strikes with more effect from this side of the Romantic movement. 'Trouble and grief'—is this what Mozart meant? Maybe, but not in any easy, superficial self-revealing way. What he uncovered herein was the general pattern of spiritual experience, beyond the reach of words.

❨ JOSEF HAYDN (1732–1809) · As Bach and Handel, so are Haydn and Mozart inseparably associated. In the case of the former pair their unconscious pursuit of the principle *divide et impera* has brought no serious consequent partisanship. The one excelled in certain fields, the other in others. Mozart and Haydn, however, occupied much of the same territory. The result is that Haydn is underrated as symphonist.

Haydn was writing symphonies, if not before Mozart was born, at any rate during his infancy. He was writing symphonies after Mozart's death. In all he has left more than a hundred, stretching over a period of nearly forty years. The earliest of these symphonies hardly count as such: the latest of them, the 'London' symphonies of 1794, are among the most notable examples of symphonic invention. What in fact did Haydn achieve in this long career? He was responsible for the classical form of symphony, for the full realization of symphonic design through an imaginative grasp of instrumental sonorities. He humanized court music by continually referring to his own peasant origins—to the music of his native Croatia—and by releasing emotional power from harmonic coloration. To what extent human emotions affected Mozart's symphonies one may never be sure. Haydn leaves us in no doubt.

It is stated by Stendhal (the material being derived from Haydn's first biographer Carpani) that Haydn—as later Elgar—noted themes in sketchbooks as apt to particular moods, so that in due course they were available for the fuller representation of these moods. Also he frequently allowed narrative to condition his composition: now it would be a tale of adventure on the high seas, now an imaginary dialogue between Christ and a repentant sinner, now the parable of the Prodigal Son.

In this there is nothing improbable—and there are sufficient titles to carry one into the ambit of Haydn's playful affection— the 'Mercury' symphony (No. 43), the 'Farewell' (No. 45), the 'Chase' (No. 73), the 'Bear' (No. 82), the 'Hen' (No. 83), the 'Surprise' (No. 94), the 'Clock' (No. 101) and any number of others.

Haydn was no devotee of aesthetic theory. For him the guiding principle was that music should give pleasure. And the circumstances of his life—most of which was spent in the congenial environment of Esterház—encouraged this. But Haydn was a devout Christian, and his first aim in life was to serve God. Thus he was obliged never to debase his standards. Composition was a ritual. Before embarking on a symphony he dressed carefully, put on the diamond ring sent to him by Frederick II, and worked only on the finest and whitest manuscript paper. A rare and lovable character, it is small wonder that his symphonies are as they are.

INTIMATE MUSIC · The passage of time, the growth of *public* interest in music, the formalities of the concert all help to obscure one feature of Haydn: his privacy. Mozart lived in the public eye and trained himself to that life. Haydn, on the other hand, preferred his country retreat, only coming into the cities—of Vienna, Paris, London (which are especially associated with his symphonies), when he could not avoid it. That he is the greatest of writers of chamber music, the maker of the string quartet— which he envisaged as a conversation between four intelligent deople—is no accident. And his symphonies are full of intimacies. A little against the principle that music is best heard 'live' I would suggest that Haydn's symphonies, especially the earlier ones, are companionable in solitude. At least one should belong to the 'desert island discs' category. And that, I think, would have gratified the composer whose breadth of vision is by no means in ratio to his distaste for travel. Haydn was sensitive to any new experience, however trivial, and it is a twin capacity for wonderment, as expressed in his slow movements, and enjoyment, the mark of his ebullient finales, that distinguishes him as the true pioneer of musical Romanticism.

As a young man Haydn was employed to write music for the house-parties of Carl von Fürnberg. He wrote divertimenti, cassations, nocturnes. Some were scored for string quartet, some for strings with wind; it depended on who was available. As a rule these works comprised five movements, of which two were minuets. Occasionally such works passed as symphonies (Op. 1 No. 5, in three movements only, for instance, was so published), so that there was no clear distinction between chamber and orchestral music. Before he took up his appointment at Esterház in 1761, Haydn composed perhaps some thirty works designated as symphonies.

PROGRAMME WORKS · At Esterház the orchestral resources were greater, and the Prince was one who employed a band not merely for prestige but because he was ardently interested in music. Thus Haydn had every incentive. Then came the distinction between the quartet and the symphony; the latter now being a congenial medium for instrumental experimentation. The symphonies divided into two groups: those, *Lamentatione* (No. 26), *Trauersymphonie* (No. 44), and *La Passione* (No. 49), which served some ecclesiastical purpose; and those which were entirely secular (c.f. *sonata di chiesa* and *sonata di camera*). In the latter Haydn was quick to indulge his fancy: hence the summing-up of the daily round in *Le Matin* (No. 6), *Le Midi* (No. 7), and *Le Soir* (No. 8). As a means of direct communication the symphony was not without its value, as is shown by the utility of the 'Farewell' symphony (No. 45).

Of the symphonies of the mid-1770's the most readily available are *L'Impériale* (No. 53), the symphony in G (No. 54), and *Il distratto* (No. 60). In these works these stylistic features are clear: a slow introduction (relevant to the title when there is one); a slow movement based on air and variation form; a robust minuet; a delight in sudden changes of key; sparkling counterpoint. And, more than is the case with Mozart, the melodies are in themselves significant. Nor do they always fall into regular four-bar units.

IN PARIS AND LONDON · After 1780, Haydn's music became known far beyond Esterház and Vienna, through the interest of Artaria, the publisher. There were other publishers, too, who were interested—in Paris, Amsterdam, London, and elsewhere. So it was that the directors of the *Concert de la Loge Olympique* in Paris engaged Haydn to write for them six symphonies (Nos. 82-7). Of these six symphonies (which included *L'Ours* and *La Poule*) the best known is *La Reine*; so called because of its approbation by Queen Marie Antoinette.

The slow movement of *La Reine* is a charming set of variations on a chanson—'La gentille et jeune Lisette'—a nice compliment to the French audience. This is an engaging example of Haydn's neatness in execution, and also of his fancy. Note the pellucidity of the scoring, the delicacy of the writing for horns, bassoons, oboes, and flute. As for the first movement it nicely illuminates Haydn's taste for phrases of odd length: the slow introduction shows 3 +3 +4 bars, while the *vivace* commences with 4 +4 +3. A further feature of the opening movement is the close alliance between the first subject (violins) and the second (bar 78, oboe). Notice also how from bars 190–211 Haydn plays about the key of G minor, before finally deciding to call it a day and to present the recapitulation.

It is hard to pass by German art or literature of the 1780's without bringing in *Sturm und Drang*. To refer this term to Haydn it is necessary to look a little more closely at some of the slow movements, particularly, perhaps, that of the *Oxford* symphony (No. 92) of *c*. 1788. Here the sunshine of the *adagio cantabile* is shut out by the menacing clouds which accumulate with the two changes to minor tonality. A powerful, angry incident, indicating that Haydn was not unaware of the storms of life. Such episodes are the more telling in Haydn (see also *Surprise* symphony, No. 94) because of their sudden approach.

In 1790 Haydn's patron, Prince Nicolas of Esterház, died.

G

Hearing this, Salomon, the London impresario, hastened to Austria to invite Haydn to London. Haydn duly came in 1791, and again in 1794. To these visits we owe the last twelve symphonies— the 'London' symphonies, in which Haydn's greatness as symphonist is most abundantly shown. And not only Haydn's, for in these works is evidence of the impact made on the older master by the music of Mozart.

With the last great symphonies of Haydn—especially the 'Clock' (No. 101), of which the simple comedy is transmuted by exquisite colouring; the 'Military' (No. 100) in which Haydn reinforces his powerful score by the addition of clarinets; the 'Drum-roll' (No. 103), with the most exciting of Haydn's essays in variation; the 'London' (No. 104), a splendidly blended composition—an epoch ended: the age of the composer-craftsman, of the private patron. Five years after the last of Haydn's symphonies came the first of Beethoven's. But that would not have been but for the combined genius of Haydn and Mozart.

VII. Beethoven's Successors

¶ A MISCELLANY OF SYMPHONISTS · For reasons which are obvious the odds were heavily against the survival of symphonies that were markedly inferior to those of Haydn, Mozart, and Beethoven. But that there were other symphonists, some with fine standards of technique, others with high ideals, and some with both, is a fact that should not be overlooked. Besides, the by-ways of music often repay sympathetic attention. One day, no doubt, scholars will shower devotion on the lesser composers of the Beethoven era, and then works which occasionally (and properly) break the routine performances of amateur societies will reach the catalogues of recorded music.

Lest it be thought that Beethoven symphonized in solitary splendour it should be recorded that in Paris—a city not generally thought symphony-conscious—there were three considerable figures; in Gossec—that worthy nonagenarian who, only two years younger than Haydn, actually outlived Beethoven—Méhul, and Cherubini.

The music of Gossec at one time had attracted the keen ear of Mozart. Classical in manner, his symphonies are intrepid music with a vitality of their own. In other works Gossec experimented considerably. His symphonies, however, clearly belong to the eighteenth century. But we should be cautious. For the symphonies of Gyrowetz, a Bohemian composer who also lived to a great age and outlasted Mendelssohn, also appear impeccably classical. Yet Burney's friend the Reverend Thomas Twining noted in these very works 'a something of his own, mixed with the improvement which every man must owe to his predecessors in the art'.

Méhul and Cherubini, who were prominent as opera composers, were both highly regarded by Beethoven as exemplary and serious composers and as innovators in the field of instrumental tone-colour. A rather stiff manner, however, does not obscure the depth of their feeling. As evidence there may be adduced Cherubini's symphony in D, composed for the Philharmonic Society of London in 1815, and now recorded. In passing it may be noted that in 1829 Cherubini re-scored this symphony for string quartet, thus drawing attention to the conviction that line and mass mattered in the form of music more than 'colour'. Cherubini was regarded as a great academician.

❡ JAN VACLAV TOMAŠEK (1774–1850) and MUZIO CLEMENTI (1752–1832) · Tomašek and Clementi, whose little immortality centres on their piano music, also wrote symphonies. Tomašek was an early nationalist, while Clementi attempted to infuse into his symphonies some aspects of nineteenth-century feeling. Four symphonies by Clementi, not all complete, are in the library of Congress at Washington, and two have been edited by Alfredo Casella, who reveals that 'side by side with pages of a Haydn-esque quality, one finds others which suggest Beethoven and even hint prophetically at Verdi and Brahms'. Clementi also outlived Beethoven.

❡ LOUIS SPOHR (1784-1859) · Rather more notable, for he commanded European attention by his virtuoso violin technique, his skill in conducting, his ambition and mastery as a composer, and his great knowledge of music, is Louis Spohr. Like Beethoven he wrote nine symphonies. Like Beethoven he had an individual style. But his reputation waned when it was seen that he was too much a victim of his own mannerisms. He lacked rhythmic incisiveness and variety, and effectual chromatic turns of phrase that once heard are never forgotten. In short, Spohr tends to tedium. His symphonies, however, show as well as those of Beethoven which way the wind was blowing.

Spohr's fourth symphony, composed in 1832, was entitled *Die Weihe der Töne*, and based on a poem by Marianne Pfeiffer. The poem was intended either to be set in the programme, or read aloud at the time of performance. An illustrative work, *Die Weihe der Töne* departs considerably from the formal symphonic plan, being in effect a sequence of episodes. Among subsequent symphonies of Spohr were the *Historische* (No. 6), *Irdisches* and *Göttliches im Menschenleben* (No. 7), for two orchestras, and *Die Jahreszeiten* (No. 9).

In the music of Spohr one is reminded of similar composers of a century later. Ambitious works (see Scriabin) with earnest intentions, for a time in vogue, but quickly dropped. The reason for this rapid obsolescence seems to lie in a spurious modernity and a deficiency in basic musical values.

❲ FRANZ SCHUBERT (1797–1828) · Which brings us to the symphonies of Schubert. Two, if not three, of these are outside temporal considerations. It does not matter when the 'Unfinished' and 'Great C major' symphonies were composed. They are at all times both new and old.

At the present time musical education is much talked about. The progress towards creative consummation is through textbooks and examinations. At the age of sixteen or seventeen it is possible that the really promising pupil is well enough versed in the technique of an age other than his own. It is also possible that he (or she) may have listened to a fair amount of music; one may even expect him to have taken part in orchestral playing. But that he shall have written pieces—let alone symphonies—for the school orchestra to play is, in general, too much to expect. And if, happily, the exception is met it is highly improbable that the resultant work will bear much relation to contemporary style. Does it matter? I venture to think so. We turn back to Schubert.

The dominant characteristic of Schubert's music is its naturalness, its inevitability. To alter a note here or there is to destroy this inevitability. So much may easily be proved by trial and error. The conclusion is that Schubert knew what he was about.

A composer will fall into one of two categories. Either he will be one whose determination is to demonstrate a thesis—such as, the country is a good place (see most 'Pastoral' symphonies); or, tonality is bunk: or he may be more content to pick up the raw material of music, shape it, and express delight in the beauty of music. Art for art's sake is not always quite so silly as it sounds.

Schubert's genius lay primarily in his capacity to make music that was in itself beautiful. *Die Weihe der Töne*: the consecration of sound. Spohr had intentions in the same direction, but lacked Schubert's unselfconsciousness. A pedant—which in his way Spohr was—will never quite be free from the desire to justify himself by proof. Schubert's symphonies *are*: they exist in their own right and independent of other considerations.

The Convict, or Imperial Seminary, in Vienna, which was Schubert's school, included a good deal of music in its scheme of education. The emphasis was on doing rather than on knowing. Choirboys were supplied to the Imperial Court Chapel, and there was (as in all self-respecting German and Austrian schools) an orchestra. For this Schubert, aged sixteen, wrote his first symphony. And it was to the headmaster of the Seminary that the second symphony was dedicated.

Not epoch-making works, but evidences of an awareness of what was happening in the larger world of music and more expertly scored than one has a right to expect from a schoolboy viola player. For the next year or two Schubert continued to compose symphonies, for the amateur band that collected at Otto Hatwig's house.

Before he was twenty-one Schubert had written six symphonies. From these it is clear that he was acquainted with the scores of Mozart, Haydn, Beethoven, Méhul, Weber, and other composers. In form, in details of instrumental layout, in harmonic colouring all this is apparent.

But there was something more. Schubert's melodies were not

all from common stock; his manipulation of tonal contrasts promised new enchantment; his ebullience—Viennese if you like—was infectious. The first high-water mark was the fifth symphony in B flat. The 'Tragic' symphony of the same year had gone off rather at half-cock; original in occasional details (especially harmonic), but neither convincingly 'tragic' nor yet wholly symphonic.

The repetitiousness that mars the 'Tragic' has, however, no place in the fifth symphony. Here is a brilliant example of Schubert's faculty for the organization of sound. The pattern and scope of the melodies, the manner of their treatment, fit perfectly within the framework of the orchestration. The scoring is for a small ensemble—without clarinets, trumpets, or drums.

Among the felicities of this symphony are the sly entry of the recapitulation action of the first movement by way of E flat major; the transformation wrought in the slow movement by the shift to C flat major; the rhythmic structure of the minuet and trio, the relation of their keys to that of the whole work, the *insouciance* of the last movement. And the melodies are ineradicable from the memory.

THE 'UNFINISHED' · It is, however, on the eighth and ninth symphonies that Schubert's symphonic reputation primarily depends. These are by all standards great works. It is sobering to know that Schubert himself never heard them. The eighth—the 'Unfinished'—was intended for the Styrian Musical Society at Graz, of which Schubert was made an honorary member in 1823. Forty-two years later (the score of the two completed movements having been all that time in the possession of the director of the Society) the first performance was given. The ninth symphony, written in 1828, was among the effects preserved by Ferdinand Schubert. It was Schumann who discovered it in 1838, and arranged for its publication and its performance by Mendelssohn at a Gewandhaus concert in Leipzig.

Note the dates of composition in relation to Beethoven's career. By the 1820's both Beethoven and Schubert had assimilated the content of German Romantic thought and the late symphonies of both are an exposition of their realization of the

Romantic attitude. Without derogation Beethoven interpreted
the didactic impulse; Schubert the naturalistic. This is why there
is no comparison, no collision. This is why the first reaction *how
beautiful* is the proper response to Schubert.

I would almost go so far as to state that the opening of the
slow movement of the 'Unfinished' symphony is the most immediately beautiful moment in music. From this impossible position discretion bids a retreat. But to hedge it round with qualifica-
tions is equally impossible. Let us see what happens.

From a *pianissimo* chord of E major, in close formation, the
horns and bassoons on the one hand, the *pizzicato* basses on the
other unfold. At the third bar the string family shed new and
ethereal light on the same tonal centre. The cellos, we notice, are
melodically employed. The same pattern is repeated, but flutes
and clarinets enter, fiddles and bassoons flutter through a bar of
semi-quavers. If the term 'impressionistic' had not been cornered
by a later school one would vouch for the impressionism—the
play of light and shadow—of this music. Before long, however,
the clarinet (how well German and Austrian composers understood the quality of this instrument) introduces a second theme,
offset by a more troubled rhythm in the strings. There are two
propositions; the basis of sonata-style dialectic. Impressionism,
after all, won't do. Yet the argument, the development of the
music, is never far from this definition for the changes of harmonic and instrumental colour are magical.

It is, of course, the first movement of this symphony which is
'famous'. Darkness and light; B minor (cellos and horns; agitated
violins; oboe and clarinet) and G major (cellos and then violins
against a comfortable off-the-beat pattern). But after the qualities
that fitted into *Lilac Time* are those which only belong to the
artist with the symphonic view. In short, the handling of the
emotional overtones of the basic themes. Note the climaxes, the
rhythmic variations, the intermittent points of suspense. The
first movement has great strength. After such dynamism the slow
movement arrives with intensity. And after the rigours of B
minor the new tonality of E major is entirely *féerique*. So one sees
how relationships make music; not the single theme, nor the

isolated tonality—but each in contrast to, or communion with, the other.

'GREAT' C MAJOR · Composers vary in method, as in outlook. Some—Beethoven, for example—will take material as unpromising (or as promising) as a bare fifth and work, sculptor-like, according to its hidden patterns. Others are embarrassed by surrounding fertility. Schubert—the composer of six hundred songs—could not avoid tunes. So we find in the 'Great' C major symphony, which, surely, has some claim to ranking as the most tuneful symphony in existence.

The opening of the symphony is more than tuneful. It is significant—a solemn line announced by the horn. Significant of what? To this there is no answer. In this instance Schubert, though clearly not unaware of the temper of the symphonic Beethoven, is the musician *pur sang*; and the solemnity is immediately enwrapped in a glory of orchestral colouring. The whole movement is bound by this initial melody which, appearing in full majesty at the movement's end, forms an envelope. Of this the contents are ebullience (see the first subject at bar 79) and fancy (see the second subject at bar 134).

The mainsprings of music are song and dance. In this movement—indeed in the whole symphony—the two are one. So, in a philosophical sense, the work is comprehensive—which is what a mature symphony should be.

The second movement, in character and outline, pays tribute to the Beethoven ethos. It is a march, and ranges between sadness and consolation (note the benignity of the music as from bar 93). Herein one would come down fairly heavily on the Romantic side—there is an irresistible emotional stimulus in the music itself, there is the famous interrogatory passage where horns hold firm in a doubtful harmonic climate (bars 168–180), there are the succeeding trumpet calls of some realistic virtue; but there is power in the organization of the material, so that what to the listener seems spontaneous and unexpected is palpably part of a preordained scheme. There is nothing irrelevant.

It is, I think, possible to discover something symbolic in this movement. Elsewhere (second subject, first movement, and the whole of the scherzo) it is common to relate the quality to the spirit of Vienna. But Vienna had its two aspects: it should be remembered that war left its hideous trail across the lifetime of Schubert. In the second movement is there not some hint of this?

But music was more important to Schubert than people or places. So it is that the symphonies as a whole, and this in particular, tell us nothing of the composer himself. It is an aspiring work: if about life then about a spiritual life. Schubert had this in common with Mozart. 'Reality' has been hinted at because of a common conception of music as relating the personal feelings of its creator—sad music, sad mood; gay music, gay mood; and so on.

A great composer lives dangerously in more ways than one. Both the third and fourth movements of the ninth symphony of Schubert are breath-taking at their start. How is the pace maintained? In both cases by rhythmic details which generate their own energy. Carried by the controlled impetuosity of the rhythms the listener passes from one tract of melodic invention to another. The delight in changing scenery is communicated by a superb command of instrumental sonorities on the one hand, and by a never-failing genius for throwing new light on a familiar object by subtle changes of key. Of these (and they are many) the most outstanding and most obvious is the switch from C major to A major for the trio of the scherzo. Note how inevitable this is. The horns pronounce the single note E twenty-four times. This note is essential to C major (as the *major third* of the *tonic* chord), but also (as *dominant*) to A major.

MUSIKVEREIN OF VIENNA · When the Musikverein of Vienna first attempted this last symphony of Schubert in 1828 they speedily dismissed it as 'too difficult'. And when, sixteen years later, Mendelssohn induced the Philharmonic Society in London to attempt it the band staged a strike. So is great music—of necessity ahead of its time in some particulars at least—regarded by some. (Not, of course, that the reverse is true: that discontent is an absolute mark of greatness.)

One can see one way in particular in which this symphony represented a new point of view. The *quality* of the sound is important. Attention has been drawn to the horns; but the ear is captured by the felicity of the music assigned to every department of the orchestra. So, particularly, one catches the essential value of the trombones in the score; which are employed not solely to make more noise, but to unveil fresh regions of beauty. The classic instance is the progress of the trombones from bar 199 of the first movement until the music settles on dominant harmony some thirty bars later. Or we can study the function of the brass in the second movement.

❡ SOME PIONEER ORCHESTRAS · The colour of the orchestra—as something in itself. That is an appreciable point at the present time, where the orchestra (and its conductor) often seems more important than the music it conveys. The process of making the means more significant than the end started a little more than a century ago. Among the orchestras which are distinguished at the present time these, then, began their modern function of playing to large audiences in large and often newly built concert halls: the Royal Philharmonic Society of London; the Vienna Philharmonic Orchestra; the New York Philharmonic Orchestra; the Orchestra of the Leipzig Gewandhaus; the Orchestra of the Paris Conservatoire Concerts; the Hallé Orchestra. Some of these orchestras grew from existing organizations, some were taken from opera houses. But, independently, they were able to lay before their audiences new and exciting standards of virtuosity.

What Berlioz wrote in 1845, in his *Memoirs*, of the orchestra in Vienna (directed by Otto Nicolai, now remembered only by his *Merry Wives of Windsor*) has an up-to-date flavour: 'they are first class. . . . Besides its assurance, its temper, and perfect technical skill, this orchestra has a singular beauty of timbre achieved without doubt, by the purity of each individual instrument and the absence of any wrong intonation.' In addition Berlioz noted an absence of vanity, and a devotion to musicianship that were altogether remarkable.

The development of orchestras in the nineteenth century (rather later than those already mentioned came the great orchestras of Prague, Berlin, Amsterdam, Boston, Chicago and Philadelphia) can be seen as the consequence of two impulses. 'Colour' was an ingredient of Romanticism—and the orchestra had all the colours available to the ear. And the enjoyment of music was, if not as universal as the popular educators would have liked, pretty general among the middle classes. The arch-duke, the princeling, the cardinal was no longer the chief patron and arbiter of taste, but—the 'public'.

The conductor of today is, often, regarded as a musical 'public relations officer'. But, in general, he is no longer a composer. The last of the considerable composer-conductors was Mahler. The first was Mendelssohn. The expertness of Mendelssohn as an orchestral composer shows up in every work: especially in comparison with those of his friend and contemporary Schumann. Mendelssohn knew exactly what he wanted to say, and how to say it. Schumann, on the other hand, knew—more or less—what he wanted to say, but—orchestrally—was in doubt in regard to its proper expression. Temperament particularly affected these composers. Mendelssohn, clear, precise, objective, had classical affinities, though living in a Romantic era. Schumann was the complete Romantic.

❡ FELIX MENDELSSOHN (1809–1847) · Mendelssohn (who in boyhood wrote a dozen light-weight symphonies for small orchestra) was an able exponent of classical design—even if in the third symphony he toyed with the idea of further unification by using as a basic theme that which the oboe plays at the outset. He was indeed one of the impeccable stylists—which fact is nowhere better exemplified than in the fourth symphony.

There was, however, the spirit of the age. Music in the 1830's and 40's had its duty to the outside world. So one symphony, all light and movement, is termed 'Italian'; another, of more sober cast, 'Scottish'. In the former the slow movement, a 'pilgrims' march', veers towards narrative, and the *finale* catches more of the *genius loci* in an informative *Saltarello*. The 'Scottish' symphony (a neglected work) turns northward in tonality (A minor) and tunes its jovialities to the pentatonic scale. In the 'Reformation' Symphony Mendelssohn, celebrating the quatercentenary of the inauguration of the Lutheran faith, based the last movement on the chorale melody of *Ein' feste Burg*. While beyond the purely instrumental symphonies there was the *Lobgesang*, another 'occasional' work, first performed in St Thomas's Church, Leipzig, in 1840, in celebration of the invention of printing.

Now Mendelssohn was too complete a musician not to be worth listening to. His technique is secure, and notable for its economy; and his scoring, as befits the most distinguished orchestral director of the time, immaculate. Whether the music 'says anything' is another matter. The slow movements probably don't, for Mendelssohn's temperament was notably volatile; but for the rest, it may be felt that he declares a faith in the orderliness of music. Not for nothing was he a classical scholar, and it is perhaps not inappropriate that the 'Italian' symphony is that which makes a particular virtue of clarity. Yet in the final movement of this work there is also a touch of astringency.

Mendelssohn, of course, was a brilliant executive musician and a fine administrator. Perhaps his genius found its greatest outlet in making opportunities for others to study music (in Leipzig, and Berlin), and in impressing the value of music on European culture. Composition was one activity among many.

❡ ROBERT SCHUMANN (1810–1856) · With Schumann it was otherwise. Here was the dedicated composer. In some ways he was the arch-Romantic, for music was an exposition of mystical affinities—with people, with nature, with the Almighty. Music with a message can be very dull. Schumann's sometimes is. So, apart from certain perfunctory centenary tributes, his symphonies have not of late been much in the public ear. That is a pity—on the one hand because Schumann's intense musicality could not fail to reveal new possibilities, on the other because his mind, singularly naïve in some respects, overlaps the common mind. That is to say, that his approach to musical creation is that of many who would like to be composers but (for many reasons) can't, and we may well persuade ourselves on listening to Schumann that that is the way in which we 'feel'.

It is a paradox that Mendelssohn, who could afford to be a dilettante, was the paragon of professionals; while Schumann, who needed to support a large family on his earnings, was almost entirely without professional competence. The notable points about Schumann are these: he worshipped Schubert, Beethoven, and Bach—whose influence is evident in melodic fancy, ambitious and philosophic concepts, and in a rehabilitated contrapuntal expression; he was an ardent student of the poets and novelists of the Romantic era in Germany; he was schizophrenic. The original quality of his music lies in its apparent frequent perception of the background of mental behaviour. Attention may be drawn to the long and intense introduction of the second symphony, and to the slow movement of the same symphony; and to the polyphonic dignity of the fourth movement of the third symphony. In these passages is a largeness of utterance which, recollecting the manner of Bach in a technical sense, carries unmistakably the marks of suffering that distinguish the tragic quality of great art.

Schumann's first symphony, to which form he turned after his previous concentration on pianoforte music and songs, was inspired by a poem by Adolph Böttger. It is a programme piece—about 'Spring'. So far so good. Spring awakens at the outset in a horn and trumpet 'motto theme' (c.f. Schubert's in the C major symphony). And after 'Spring's Awakening' come the subsequent movements, at first entitled (but the titles were withheld from publication) 'Evening', 'Merry Playmates', and 'Spring's Farewell'. Of purely musical interest is the manner in which the serene melody of the second movement derives from the 'motto theme', and the transformation of a tail-end tune in this movement into the principal theme of the scherzo.

In his D minor symphony (written in 1841) but revised and published as No. 4 ten years later) this thematic economy is more conspicuous. The figure which appears at once in the second violins and violas—their tone thickened by the bassoons—reappears in the slow movement (characteristically called *Romanza*) and in the scherzo. While the 'baroque' pattern first heard from the first violins in bar 22 of the introduction forms the main substance of the finale. In the C major symphony the introduction, to which attention has already been drawn, is quoted at three later points—at the conclusion of the first, second, and fourth movements;

while the second subject of the finale is based on the first four notes of the second subject.

In many ways the most attractive of Schumann's symphonies, the third, the 'Rhenish', is diffusely unsymphonic. There are five movements. The first, of great length, is abundantly energetic and rhythmically progressive; the second mixes beer-garden *camaraderie* with quaintly humorous contrapuntal interludes; the third is a song without words (Schumann's lyrical gift is never long absent from his symphonies); the fourth the solemnity devised after visiting Cologne Cathedral at the time of the enthronement of a cardinal; the fifth a gallant, if somewhat ponderous, expression of good cheer.

Why are these symphonies neglected? The reason is twofold. They are not orchestrated with, say, Mendelssohn's efficiency, and accordingly provide interpretative problems for conductors whose solutions cannot lead to evident virtuosity. They have been rescored by Mahler, but have not made much headway in this form. Which leads to the other obstacle. Schumann, despite his attempts to unify symphonic form, rarely succeeded in embracing any one symphony within a unity of purpose. And this is where Brahms may be seen to succeed where Schumann, his friend and mentor, failed.

⟨ JOHANNES BRAHMS (1833–1897) · As symphonists Mendelssohn and Schumann subscribed to the symphonic ideal: that the music should enjoy its own life as music. But pictorial and literary values are never quite excluded. And what is not in the music may be subjectively restored by the tissues of association. In the case of Brahms it is irrelevant how he lived; what he read; what, apart from his creative function, he did. Nor was Brahms conspicuously affected by the ebb and flow of fashion. His symphonies are in the grand tradition—independent and self-sufficient.

SERENADES · Before embarking on the symphonies, however, the listener might well become acquainted with the two Serenades which Brahms wrote at Detmold, at the age of twenty-five. As Professor Altmann says these should be restored to the general repertoire; if for no other reason than to show that Brahms actively *enjoyed* music—in the way that Haydn and Mozart did. It was at

Detmold that Brahms, in tranquillity and at ease after the turmoil of his chequered youth, first seriously studied the symphonies, divertimenti, and serenades of Haydn and Mozart. Op. 11 and Op. 16 are truly serenades, each of five movements, of which one was a scherzo.

It is sometimes suggested that Brahms was indifferent to instrumental colouring: the denial of that is in these works, the second holding additional interest on account of the exclusion of violins. And what a lovely opening there is to the first, with solo horn descanting above a drone bass, to be followed by a congenial repetition of the horn tune by clarinet. Throughout these works horns and clarinets speak with an eloquence learnt from Mozart, Beethoven, and Weber. Otherwise may be noticed the rhythmic flexibility which Brahms learned from Schumann but developed beyond Schumann's capacity; the enharmonic key changes that came also by way of Schumann, but from Schubert; and the purposefulness that hints at an inflexible will even in the smallest movement. What could be more Brahmsian than the mysterious octaves of the scherzo of the first Serenade, or the careful counterpoint of the *Adagio non troppo* of the second? Or who but Brahms could have invested a minuet with such severe meaning as is implicit in the *quasi menuetto* of the second?

⁋ SYMPHONIES · It was exciting to be alive in the early 1860's. Music-lovers abreast of the times were acquainted with the symphonic poems and 'Dante' and 'Faust' symphonies of Liszt; *Béatrice et Bénédict*, and *Les Troyens* by Berlioz; *Un ballo in maschera*, *La forza del destino*, and *Les Vêpres Siciliennes* by Verdi; *Tannhäuser* by Wagner; as well as works by Gounod, Offenbach, and Rubinstein. To be up-to-date: that was the thing then as now. Alternatively, one might not unprofitably follow the German *kapellmeisterisch* tradition and compose as correctly as Hiller, or the once so-promising Gade, or Sterndale Bennett. Gade composed six symphonies. Hiller three, Bennett (whose composition was often done in a cab from one engagement to another) one. How many symphonies they wrote is immaterial: they are buried. NO. 1 · Brahms was not one of your slick, fluent, ephemeral writers. He agonized over his work—as indeed had Beethoven.

What began sometimes as a work for one medium ended as for another. Under the aegis of the Schumanns, Brahms had begun a symphony in D minor in 1854. But this changed direction and was ultimately transformed from the two-piano form in which it had been sketched; two movements into the first piano concerto; and one—a funeral march—into the second movement of the *Requiem*. Twenty-two years later the first symphony in C minor appeared. 'Seldom, if ever', wrote Hanslick, 'has the entire musical world awaited a composer's first symphony with such tense anticipation—testimony that the unusual was expected of Brahms in this supreme and ultimately difficult form.'

'Do you know', said Brahms on one occasion, 'there are asses in Vienna who take me for a second Beethoven?' That this could be the case was symptomatic of a lacuna in the music of the 1870's. Brahms appeared to understand the fundamentals of music in a way which his contemporaries did not. So (even if his works did not win quick, popular success—indeed the 'difficulties' of his style incensed many, who were quick to voice disapproval) the first symphony was observed to centre on large issues.

The introduction to the first movement is of titanic proportion. Dark, restless, and for ever striving, its angularities of melody, complexity of counterpoint and rhythm, communicate themselves to the movement proper. This may be seen as the determination of a master to subdue refractory musical material to his will, or, more poetically, as 'Faustian conflicts'. In the second movement Brahms draws on his experience as a song-writer. Despite the superficial resemblances with Mendelssohn, however, this is no 'song without words' but a representation of lyrical thought in instrumental—and symphonic—language. There should be noted the particular effect of brightness and beauty wrought by the solo violin which rides over the score from bar 90 onwards. The third movement is unexpected. In place of a scherzo is a brief movement in A flat which moves away from the *andante sostenuto* of its predecessor, but no further than *un poco allegretto*. In character it resembles the more innocent of the *Variations on a theme of Haydn* (performed in 1874); but the middle section, in B major, throws thought back to the endeavours

H

of the first movement. The finale of this symphony is, of course, one of the notable symphonic finales. The long, strenuous, questing introduction is as full of suspense as music can be. There must, we say, be a solution to this. At bar 30 the clouds begin to clear. The horn call against the muted background of *tremolo* strings summons the theme of the *allegro non troppo, ma con brio*. 'The entrance of the *Allegro*, with its simple, beautiful themes, reminiscent of the "Ode to Joy" in the Ninth Symphony, is overpowering as it rises onward and upward, right to the end.' So Hanslick summarized this triumph song.

NO. 2 · The first symphony was performed for the first time at Carlsruhe in November 1876. In the summer of the following year the second symphony was composed in Carinthia. Brahms was delighted with his surroundings: they were, he said, 'charming and delightful' and he was conscious of a characteristically 'Austrian cosiness and kindheartedness'. Under such conditions, and in reaction against the rigours of the first, exhausting symphony, the first movement of the second symphony came out 'merry and tender, as though specially written for a newly married couple'. We are returned to the prevailing mood of the Serenades and able to reflect on the geniality of Haydn. But if in every melodic contour there is an engaging simplicity this is deceptive. For the whole work is wide in emotional range and expression. Consider, for instance, the varied rhythmic and tonal antitheses of the scherzo; the scholar-poet's rumination on the motivs of the finale. A tuneful symphony. So it is, and with an Austrian flavour: but see what Brahms does with the tunes. What he does is so pellucid that comment is superfluous.

NO. 3 · The third symphony was christened—not altogether aptly —Brahms's 'Eroica' by Richter, who conducted its first performance at a Philharmonic Concert in Vienna in December 1883. This is a tense, dark work, with the climax reserved for the last movement (of which the dark, mysterious, moving octaves recall the early deposition of this sort of idea in the Serenade in D). It is a feature of Brahms's symphonies that his last movements are dramatically conclusive, and this goes some way to explain the deliberate curtailment of the middle movements—which were once thought to be inadequate. But if Brahms knew how to end a symphony he also knew how to begin. So in the third symphony there is another of those commanding gestures in the grand manner. F, A flat, F: a three-note motiv, from which all else emerges.

NO. 4 · The fourth and last symphony, composed in 1884 and 1885, was performed for the first time by the Meiningen Orchestra (the last of the Court orchestras of Germany) in the autumn of the latter year. Brahms alluded to the character of the music in a letter to Hans von Bülow—'I fear it smacks of the climate of this country—the cherries are not sweet here and you would certainly not eat them.' As usual he was doubtful of the reception it would get; perhaps more than usually doubtful, for the music was of even more austere quality. (The other prominent symphonists of the 1880's, each more obviously aware of the 'spirit of the age', were Bruckner and Dvořák.)

The austerity may now be less evident than seventy years ago, but, nevertheless, we still brace ourselves for the cerebration of a passacaglia—which is the form adopted by Brahms for his last movement. And what a splendid movement it is. The idea of a 'note-row' is by no means new. The reiterated bass—or ground bass—was, of course, a formal device in favour in the seventeenth and eighteenth centuries.

A wise listener will hear Bach's great organ passacaglia in C minor and compare the Brahmsian method of tackling the same problem. He will perhaps also make the effort to hear a similar movement in the E minor organ sonata (Op. 132) of Rheinberger (a contemporary of Brahms). Rheinberger was also in the van of the back-to-Bach movement which has subsequently enveloped almost every composer of intellectual parts.

The theme of Brahms's movement is indeed quoted from Bach's 150th Church Cantata. The distance between Rheinberger and Brahms is to be measured in units of imagination. Rheinberger's passacaglia is a fine work. That of Brahms is great —for in his case the fundamental theme throws off poetic observations that cannot be anticipated—in the way in which the details of competent craftsmanship can. Notice, for example, the counter-

melody of the fourth variation which is so evidently in accord
with the mood of the first movement; the flute solo, in which lies
the shape of the theme, of variation 12; the solemn trombone
chorus of variations 14 and 15; the abounding coda, which is
variation 30.

At this point one is aware of the quality of Brahms's orchestration. The instrumentation is at one with the content of the musical
thought. And this can be traced throughout the symphonic
works, from the early Serenades. Brahms wrote no young person's guide to the orchestra, but the finale of the fourth symphony
is a fine index to orchestral sonorities for the mature listener.

Preceding the passacaglia of the last symphony is a scherzo—
an untidy, shaggy fellow, shoved on by a full-blooded rhythmic
pattern and made the more droll by the extra piccolo, double-
bassoon, and triangle. An Aristophanic movement. If the analogy
might be carried back the slow movement is as a pastoral by
Theocritus, the first movement Aeschylean.

In short the symphony, as perhaps the other three also, stands
away from considerations of time and place. The genius of
Brahms saw the future in the past—and the past in the future. He
was in the nineteenth century but not quite of it. Which is one
interpretation of the classical ethos.

VIII. Expanding Tradition

❡ FRENCH SYMPHONISTS · It is fortunate that neither musical form nor vocabulary is controlled by edict. If they were the number of dull symphonies extant would be larger than it is. The text-books used to say that a symphony should (a) be in four movements, each of a particular order and in a particular sequence, and (b) pay close attention to 'sonata' form. And according to the text-book outline it used to be possible to fabricate such works as would satisfy university examiners. At all times, however, there were composers who refused to obey conventions. Berlioz, Bizet, Franck, in different ways were unconventional and their respective diversions from the norm of symphonic pattern emphasize the essentially Austro-German character of the form in the nineteenth century.

GEORGES BIZET (1838–1875) · Berlioz did not exactly expand the symphonic tradition. Being Berlioz he started a new one, which will be fully explored in the volume in this series which will deal with programme music. Bizet, whose symphony in C is among the enchantments of the repertoire, wrote a symphony on the way to his career in the theatre. His aim was opera, but his training (at the Paris Conservatoire) was in all directions thorough and comprehensive; so, aged seventeen, when the Prix de Rome was in view, he tried out his technique in the conventional channels.

A comparison with Schubert is apt. The genius of both composers flowered early. Their originality and spontaneity in melody and colour was undoubted. Their attitude towards music was 'natural': i.e. 'I do but sing because I must. . . .' So Bizet's symphony avoids pretentiousness. The oboe melody of the second movement resembles Nadir's 'De mon amie' in *Les Pêcheurs de perles*, the themes of the finale have a quality familiar in *Carmen*; while the pellucid scoring (with Schubert's fifth symphony hardly out of mind) enhances the general appreciation of theatrical aptness. A gay work, and in accord with the temper of the earliest symphonists to whom gaiety was the main objective.

CÉSAR FRANCK (1822–1890) · French composers have generally preferred other forms than symphony and it was thirty years after Bizet's was written (after which it was lost and not recovered until 1935) that César Franck's was presented. This work was greeted with contumely. It was 'serious', and Parisians did not want serious music thrust at them. It was not a symphony at all, for, as Ambroise Thomas pointed out, it was 'too dramatic'. One critic said that it was 'an affirmation of incompetence pushed to the lengths of a dogma'. Another questioned the composer's credentials: 'Who is this Monsieur Franck? A professor of harmonium, I believe.' Someone else protested that no proper symphony could have a cor anglais (which cannot be missed in the slow movement) in the score. Sustained by a simple faith (this was his personal character) Franck believed himself to be right and the critics wrong. That, of course, is a permanent feature of the artist-critic partnership.

Observe the course of adverse criticism: the symphony was —too serious; too chromatic; incompetent; and bizarrely scored. But at least no-one could complain that it was not different. It is when the differences are added together and viewed in perspective that this work speaks with an individual voice. In short

Franck's personality comes through. Here, however, we are in difficulties. We may not approve, or sympathize with, the personality as we interpret it—in which case the progress of the music is impeded. In different ways this matter of personality affects the consideration of most late Romantic symphony. That this is so implies the end, as well as the expansion, of a tradition.

César Franck was an organist—of the church of St Clotilde in Paris—and this vocation induced a respect for academic craftsmanship. His music is, as they say, invariably 'well put together'. It is, indeed, sometimes too consciously put together. That the symphony is 'cyclic' in design is obvious—and rather tiresomely so.

The first movement begins *lento*, with a gloomy motiv (borrowed from Liszt's *Les Préludes*) in the lower strings. This motiv carries through the introduction, and furnishes the start to the *Allegro non troppo*. Before long this subsides into the introductory *lento* section, now set in F minor. The *Allegro non troppo* again, also in F minor. From the disquiet of the first theme the movement graduates to a serener melody (strings) in F major, which leads to a second theme in the same key (19 bars after letter E).

Franck had a curious habit of melody. He would circle round one note. So it is here. Announced *fortissimo* this melody is, perhaps, irritating in its static quality. The intention was to provide the suitable contrast to the first principal melody; certainty answering doubt. Ingenious development of the themes, which goes through contrapuntal (for Franck was a great disciple of Bach) and harmonic by-ways, is followed by recapitulation of the *lento* and *allegro* sections, ingeniously diversified. In the final bars (the dynamic by now is *fff*) the first motiv is urgently stated yet again.

The second movement takes the place of the conventional two middle movements of 'classical' symphony. An intermezzo, with variations, it has affinities with Schumann. The key is dark and distant—E flat minor. Harp and strings prepare the way for the cor anglais, which makes its celebrated entry at letter [**A**], taking its initial tune-shape from that of the first motiv of the first movement. A long melody—which is eventually carried on by clarinet and horn, and which circulates through various tonalities—this serves as the subject of later variation (see letter [F], where it is diminished; and letter [M]). But setting it off are two interludes, the one in B flat (letter [C]) which catches a gentle echo of the second prominent melody of the first movement; the other, of more whimsical character, in E flat.

In the final movement—*allegro non troppo*—the characteristics are the melody in cellos and basses which appears, *dolce cantabile*, at the seventh bar and which pushes forward to a second melody (five bars after letter [C]) in B major, alternating between brass and strings; the repetition of the first theme from the second movement—now in B minor; the apotheosis of the second theme from the first movement. Thus the symphony is unified. But the main themes on which the cyclic form depends are not in themselves particularly inspiring. A little ingenious maybe. But we are back where we started; for so, too, was the composer, at heart. Thus about this symphony it might be felt by some that simple ideas have been subjected to too hyperbolic treatment. That is a reasonable point of view, but Romantic music, by its nature, is not governed by reason, and one's feelings may urge a higher regard than one's intellect.

❲ PETER TCHAIKOVSKY (1840–1893) · It was sometimes urged against Franck that his climaxes were vulgar; that his brass ensemble was overpowering. In respect of Tchaikovsky no-one has ever even troubled to deny that his music is, often, vulgar. To leave it at that, however, is insufficient. For it must be seen how the wheel has come full circle.

In its origins symphonic music was made according to the wishes of the patrons of music. That they were—or were called —aristocratic is neither here nor there. They paid for the tune, and instructed the piper what tune to play. In the first phase of Romanticism, on the other hand, the artist told his public what they were to like. (Here some of the present *avant-garde* may very well be regarded as Romantics in disguise.) In the second phase the artist once again accommodated himself to general demand. Thus in the main the late music of the nineteenth century was frankly sensational.

Now the main tradition of symphonic music is set against any form of sensationalism. Deliberately evocative colouring runs contrary to architectural planning. At the same time, however, the logical and formal scheme may be seen as a basis for literary exposition. That music exists in the dimensions of time and not of space may well be suggestive. So it was that the romantic symphonists found the conventional lay-out at least a convenience; and audiences were able to feel a degree of familiarity with music which is always agreeable.

The symphonies of Tchaikovsky are 'easier to follow' than that of César Franck, for they lack the complexity of design that distinguishes his.

In each of Tchaikovsky's six symphonies the classical pattern of sonata form is apparent. The 'cyclic' principle—as seen in Berlioz, Liszt, and Franck, is also observed—except in the first symphony. So will be noticed the consequent employment in the majority of the symphonies of introductory thematic material. The fullest use of cyclic repetition is in the fifth symphony, where the tense theme of the introduction is renewed at letter [**P**] in the third movement *Valse*, and at the beginning of the finale. Otherwise (as in the second and fourth symphonies) the initial motiv is to be found conspicuous in the 'development' section of the first movement.

In the normal course of symphonic thought repetition is not development, but rather the opposite. There is, however, another factor to be taken into consideration. Tchaikovsky was one of the greatest masters of orchestral technique, so that he will often throw new light on the character of a theme by subtle studies of colour. The texture of the music indeed is kaleidoscopic. Study, for instance, the dominating figure of the third movement of the sixth symphony, and the manner in which it is variously presented. Study also the manner in which this figure is thrown into relief by its background, and how it accumulates such energy that it forces its way to ultimate, and almost overwhelming supremacy. Could music be more *exciting*?

Tchaikovsky was pre-eminent in endowing his themes with individual character. These examples will suffice: the oboe melody in the middle section of the *scherzo* of the fourth symphony; the horn melody of the *andante cantabile* of the fifth symphony; the deathly bassoon entry at the beginning of the sixth. In melodic fertility Tchaikovsky was almost as prosperous as Schubert. But there was a difference. Tchaikovsky was aware of the implications of nationalism; of opera; and of ballet.

Less devoted to the cause of nationalism than Moussorgsky, or Borodin, or Balakirev he nonetheless based one symphony—the second, or 'Little Russian'—on folk tunes, and not infrequently imbued his original melodies with a Russian accent. As for opera the *atmosphere* of many passages, especially in the sixth symphony, is theatrical (in no derogatory sense); and no-one can fail to see Tchaikovsky the composer of ballet in the *scherzo* of the fourth symphony, or the 5/4 movement of the sixth. Of this Tchaikovsky was well aware. But, he said in answer to the criticism of his friend Taneiev, that he could 'never understand why "ballet music" should be used as a contemptuous epithet. The music of a ballet is not invariably bad, there are good works of this class— Delibes' *Sylvia* [from which perhaps came the idea for the *pizzicato* scherzo of the fourth symphony] for instance.'

Tchaikovsky was explicit as to what symphony meant to him, as he was about his defects of style. 'I have', he acknowledged, 'been much troubled all my life by my inability to grasp and manipulate form in music'. By the side, and in explanation of which, should be set his views as to function. 'I should', he wrote to Taneiev, 'be sorry if symphonies that mean nothing should flow from my pen, consisting solely of a progression of harmonies, rhythms, and modulations. Most assuredly my symphony [the fourth] has a programme, but one that cannot be expressed in words. . . . But is this not proper to a symphony, the most purely lyrical of musical forms? Should not a symphony reveal those wordless urges that hide in the heart, asking earnestly for expression?'

By which standard Tchaikovsky proved himself; for where does music otherwise so give the effect, at least, of the 'wordless urges. . . .'? In his exhibition of the emotional resources of music Tchaikovsky appears to lay himself open to inspection. There—as we read the sixth symphony—is the man. It is not thus that one feels about Berlioz, whose intention was the same. It is, of course, open to one to dislike the man-in-the-music as has been noted in the case of Franck, and then (apart from technical features which merit attention) the music is pointless. Which is where the more inscrutable classical writers—Haydn and Mozart —had the whiphand. They betrayed little interest in themselves as a source of musical inspiration.

⁋ ALEXANDER BORODIN (1833–1887) · At all times Tchaikovsky protested his Russian-ness, but his introspective temperament allied with his wide professional interests in European music as a whole took him away from the enthusiasms of his Russian contemporaries. It is to Borodin that we should look for symphonies which convey, through the statutory form, the essence of national aspiration.

In point of fact Borodin's symphonies are of somewhat earlier date than those of Tchaikovsky—and thus are nearer to the sources of nationalism. The first—in E flat—was composed between 1862 and 1867, when Borodin was much under the influence of Balakirev; the second—in B minor—between 1874 and 1877. In both symphonies one is aware of an enthusiasm that shows itself in a striking idiom (characterized by powerful rhythmic drive on the opening of the first symphony), wide range of scale (the pentatonic pattern dominates a large part of the first movement of the second symphony), and brilliance, if not bizarreness, of scoring. In common with Brahms, Borodin attached much importance to the final movements of his symphonies, which, therefore, are of generous proportion and conclusive character. It is a fine intellect which masters the lyrical and dramatic material (some of it akin to the *Prince Igor* music) of the second symphony and shows it, as through various contrapuntal devices, in symphonic capacity.

Borodin was a curious mixture of romantic and realist. He was, by profession, a chemist—professor in St Petersburg, and a research scholar. In his symphonies one feels that his ardent romanticism, so patent in *Prince Igor*, has been subjected to close scrutiny in the laboratory, thus the result is admirably objective.

When the classical symphony was in gestation influences from eastern Europe were strong. The fire, and passion, and melancholy of Borodin and Tchaikovsky were qualities once descried in the Mannheim symphonists of Bohemian origin. In the course of time these qualities were assimilated so that their separate existence ceased. Russian nationalism did a service to music in general by renewing acquaintance with a more direct manner of utterance. It was, however, Dvořák especially who exhibited the simple virtues to the greatest perfection.

❡ ANTONIN DVOŘÁK (1841–1904) · Simplicity is the mark of his symphonies. Yet with it a sense of wisdom, and a mature sympathy. Dvořák and Haydn had much in common and the symphonies of the former may well appear as a corollary to those of the older master. Of not all symphonic music can it be said that it is companionable.

This precisely describes both Haydn and Dvořák, who, inspired by a resolute faith (did they not both attribute their gifts and dedicate their works to the glory of God?), poured out music for general pleasure. It is, perhaps, unfashionable to regard aesthetic satisfaction as an end in itself. But there it is: Dvořák filtered the joy which music gave to him through his creative genius and thus passed it on, enriched by a vivid imagination. I am not sure that if I wished to proselytize among the 'unmusical' I would not turn on Dvořák's symphony in G major and leave him to do the job for me. And which part of this symphony? The answer to that is the second and third movements.

The *adagio* is an astonishing example of organic growth. The seed of the movement is within the first four notes of the melody: *me, fa, soh, lah*; part of a rising scale. The strings, urged towards emotional points of climax by gradations of tone that call for subtle interpretation, repeat the opening motiv in sequence. They pass through darker harmonies towards the key of C minor. Horns and drums momentarily hold a deep-toned C. Therefrom, at letter [A] the woodwind pick up a chord of C major, and the flute runs into it through the opening four-note motiv. But this same motiv has other suggestions. The clarinets, in thirds, take it over and, in uneasy chromatic movement, above chords in the lower strings, profess a nostalgic (or whatever adjective seems apt to the listener) mood. Clarinets and higher woodwind alternate. A descending figure by now made familiar by the first flute is caught by the strings and given a vigorous turn. This section, between [B] and [C], ends with a reflection on the opening mood of the movement, but with woodwind and horns carrying the main stream of the poetry. Between [C] and [F] lies one of the most beautifully scored passages in orchestral music. The violins had lately been silent. Now they produce a delicate pattern, in sixths, based on a descending scale. Below them the lower strings gently maintain the harmonic texture in *pizzicato* arpeggio figures. Horn, bassoons, clarinets, softly but persistently punctuate this with marks of suppressed rhythmic excitement. Above, flute and oboe sing a long, independent melody that has its origins in the commencement of the whole movement.

At [D] a solo violin takes over the melodic function and the scales are transferred from strings to woodwind. All this is worked towards a great climax in which the brass are prominent at [E]. At [F] the middle section, still in full voice, ceases abruptly: there return the end bars of the first section—formerly woodwind, now strings. The first section as a whole is now reviewed in reverse. The end of the movement is a recapitulatory presentation of the middle section, and the figure which first appeared in the flutes dies away, but now in the trumpets, across a widely spaced chord of C major.

Dvořák knew a great deal about orchestration. He had been a viola player in the Czech National Theatre. There he had come under the direction of Smetana, the influence of whose colouring may readily be discovered. In the slow movement of the G major symphony it can be seen that no player in the orchestra is insignificant. A melody in one group of instruments, a scale in another is a ready form of contrapuntal exercise. Dvořák was an artful combiner of tunes—as may also be seen in the first movement of this symphony, when the first, solemn, cello tune, and the subsequent flute melody are later joined together, with neither impeding the other.

The *scherzo* of the symphony is an *ingénue* among symphonic *scherzos*. A little sad-faced in the opening key of G minor, but the melody of the first violins quite gaily set off by the liquescent arpeggio of the woodwind; charmingly impertinent in the middle section, in which a background of national dance is revealed in the lilting rhythm; and extremely forthcoming in the coda, where the G major melody forsakes triple for double time.

Apart from his skill in dovetailing them, Dvořák's melodies have character. This is partly due to his nearness to nationalism, but partly to his conviction that melody was important. So it was that when in America he showed considerable interest in the negro spirituals which now have their place in the 'New World' symphony, and the 'Nigger' Quartet.

Smetana has been mentioned as one influence on the music of Dvořák. It is not difficult to discover also the results of his study of Beethoven (see the opening of the slow movement of the symphony in D major, Op. 60) and of Schubert. The scoring betrays also his enthusiasm for Liszt and Wagner. But in the D major symphony, especially, there is an even more obvious association. Brahms, in an unguarded moment, might have written a large part of the first movement. Dvořák admired Brahms greatly, and it was his ambition to show that symphonies of Brahmsian quality and integrity could come from Bohemia. And Brahms thought highly of Dvořák, for it was he—together with the Viennese critic Hanslick—who recommended Dvořák for a government grant in 1875. The Brahmsian conception of symphony as a musical representation of conflict with unseen forces was picked up by Dvořák in the symphony in D minor, which, in 1885, he composed for the Philharmonic Society of London. Note the gravity of the scherzo, the unquiet opening of the first movement, the passage of the last movement from doubt to certainty.

It is commonly said that Dvořák was a peasant, and remained one. In whatever degree of truth that too easy statement contains lies the endearing quality of Dvořák's music. In a period which was conspicuous for a good deal of pretentiousness in musical thought his works stand out by their ability to view musical, and emotional, situations with a clear vision.

❡ ANTON BRUCKNER (1824–1896) · Dvořák was a prolific composer, but symphonic music was a large part of his life. Two or
three symphonies are indispensable to the general stock—those
which date from his years of fame. But the complete list shows
symphonies in C minor ('The Bells of Zlonice'), composed in
1865, but lost until 1923; B flat major (1865); E flat major (1873);
D minor (1874); F major (1875, revised 1887); D major (1880);
D minor (1884-5); G major (1889); E minor ('From the New
World') (1893). Nine in all. And while Dvořák was climbing towards this goal of every symphonic composer so also was the
Austrian composer Anton Bruckner. His list comprises symphonies in C minor (1866, revised in 1891); in C minor (1872,
revised after 1880); in D minor (1873, revised 1877 and 1889); in
E flat (1874, revised 1880); in B flat (1877); in A (1881); in E
(1883); in C minor (1885, revised 1887, and 1890); in D minor,
but unfinished (1894). Beyond the statutory nine are a student
symphony in F minor, published in short score in 1932, and a
symphony in D minor, designated O (zero) and published in
revised form in 1924.

Bruckner's process of composition spread over a number of
years in the case of each of his symphonies, and often he had to
wait for more years to elapse before performances were possible.
That his works were revised drastically is suggested by the time-
table above. These revisions were made by Bruckner on the
advice of various conductors who were willing to champion his
music, but were critical of its orchestration. What manner of
composer was this, who so readily took advice? Is it not, after
all, the composer's duty to instruct the conductor?

The story of Bruckner's life has not yet been fully exploited
as a romantic fable, even though Dr Redlich has summarized its
outline in masterly fashion in his contribution on Bruckner and
Mahler to the *Master Musicians* Series (Dent).

Anton Bruckner, of peasant stock, was the son of an obscure
country schoolmaster in Upper Austria. As a chorister young
Bruckner was given his first opportunity to become acquainted
with the tradition of Austrian church music. With some capacity
for music noticeable at an early age he was instructed in the rudi-

ments of theory and organ-playing. But his career was to be that of a schoolmaster. Until the age of thirty-one he remained a schoolmaster. At the same time he acted as church organist of the cathedral at Linz, and thereafter his career as organist was distinguished.

Grinding away at composition, studying the mysteries of counterpoint and fugue, under difficult circumstances Bruckner equipped himself on the academic side so well that in 1868 he was appointed to a teaching post in the Vienna Conservatory. So far so good. And in the fullness of time Bruckner became a court organist and composer, and was decorated by the Emperor. In the brilliant society of Vienna, in the complex world of musical affairs, Bruckner, without intellectual pretensions or social graces, fitted awkwardly. He suffered many rebuffs, was despised by Brahms and the Brahmsians on account of his alleged Wagnerisms, and was rejected by all the women to whom he paid addresses. But he had a prodigious faith—in God, and in his own ability to serve God in his own way.

So much is necessary if one would listen to Bruckner sympathetically. He was a symphonist *sui generis*, for his major instrumental works sprang directly from his liturgical. The first three symphonies quote fairly extensively from his masses, and in the seventh symphony the adagio contains references to the *Te Deum*.

Bruckner's religious feelings were simple and uninhibited. When he contemplated the sacred mysteries emotion welled up from within. Such emotion demanded musical expression. His experience of music in general was slight, but Beethoven's *Choral Symphony*, Wagner's *Tannhäuser* and *Tristan*, the personalities of Liszt and Berlioz whom he met in 1865, suggested the direction his ideas should take. Before the expansive harmonic and instrumental colour ranges of these composers Bruckner discovered his proper expressive medium. Bruckner, so it has been said, had a feeling for 'the cosmic value of the chord'. So consider the opening of the fourth symphony, when a horn calls from the murmurous atmosphere sustained by the strings, of E flat major; the way in which arpeggio-shaped tunes slide across the score, the manner in which rich chordal professions follow one another in leisurely fashion; the intensification of harmonic values by ripe scoring.

One is either attracted or repelled by Bruckner's scoring. At best it is extraordinarily sonorous—like an organ, so they say, as if suggesting that organ sonorities are unmusical. As a matter of fact the *mélange* of diapasons and reeds and mutation work in a large church may be awesome. It either moves or does not move the listener. Now Bruckner does communicate something of this mystical character through his orchestration—much more impressively than Franck (who is also criticized for orchestrating like an organist). In so doing he does what he set out to do: to effect a mystical symbolism.

Austrian composers had a great love of wind instruments (note the Masses of Bruckner for voices and wind instruments which follow an ancient tradition) and Bruckner, further inspired by Wagner's example, employs them with great imagination. (In the last three symphonies he used the tubas as in Wagner's *Ring*; he increased the horns to six or eight; and enlarged the percussion department.) Note the horns in the *scherzo* of the fourth symphony, the four tubas which are solemnly prominent in the *adagio* of the seventh symphony, the flashes of brilliance from trumpets and trombones. And here we come to a distinctive feature of Bruckner's melodic idiom. His melodies often overleap normality and stretch over a large space (note the trumpet tune of the *scherzo* of the seventh symphony, the clarinet and horn tune at the beginning of the *finale* of the fourth symphony), which gesture affected Bruckner's Austrian successors.

Side by side with a love for religious things Bruckner shows a delight in country scenes. So the fourth symphony (to which Bruckner, stimulated by Liszt's extra-musical aids to understanding, affixed a programme), the 'romantic' symphony, has its pastoral associations, which are perhaps more meaningful to those who know Austria than those who do not.

The outstanding characteristic of Bruckner's (and Mahler's) symphonies are their great length—an hour and a half for the eighth symphony for example. That was the way Bruckner felt

I

and his movements are full of beautiful and original ideas. As to form; there is a point beyond which form becomes un-appreciable. An hour and a half of symphony is more than can be accepted as a unity at a sitting. But there are those who will dis-agree. Such are they whose love for Bruckner is more than a little exclusive. Hence (except in Austria where Austrian music is properly protected) the growth of Brucknerian and Mahlerian coteries.

❡ GUSTAV MAHLER (1860–1911) · Bruckner, in all essentials, is one of the last of the true Romantics. Gustav Mahler, on the other hand, who was in early life a pupil of Bruckner, is one of the first of the moderns.

At the very end of the nineteenth century Mahler was appointed conductor of the Vienna Opera, and of the Philharmonic con-certs. A ruthless taskmaster, and a high idealist, he made his orchestra (against the wishes of its members, who often bitterly resented his autocratic manner) the finest in Europe, and his pro-grammes the most enterprising. Composers given early oppor-tunity by Mahler included Hans Pfitzner, Wolf-Ferrari, and Richard Strauss, while he was partly responsible—by his inter-pretation of the fifth and sixth symphonies—for the widening of interest in Bruckner's music. It was Mahler, too, who was respon-sible for the introduction of a more authentic style than had previously obtained in respect of the operas of Mozart. Mahler became a conductor of world renown and, after many occasional engagements in America, became, in 1909, first conductor of the New York Philharmonic Society.

It is not surprising that as composer Mahler was a supreme master of orchestration. In some ways one is reminded of Berlioz. For Mahler required a vast orchestra for the expression of his romantic creed, yet employed his forces economically. Instead of loading the score in the Wagner-Bruckner manner he imparted to it an astringency that came from the isolation of certain tone colours—notably woodwind and trumpets, and new effects in percussion. The seventh symphony, the 'Tragic', amply illustrates these points. Those with an ear for 'glacial' effects may like to compare the use of cow-bells in this score with that of the percussion in the 'Landscape' movement of Vaughan Williams's *Sinfonia Antartica*. It was 'the fierce instrumentation' and the often cynical contemplation of dying Romanticism of the seventh symphony especially that inspired Mahler's disciples—Schoenberg and Berg. In his feeling for 'functional' orchestration his tonality-dissolving chromaticism, his stress on linear development Mahler pointed towards the new romanticism of the atonalists. It is to be recorded that the seventh symphony was ill-received at its first performance in 1906.

It is not, however, this work, but rather the six-movement *Das Lied von der Erde* which (through its interpretation by Kathleen Ferrier) has captivated English audiences. And here is a blend of voluptuousness, of pessimism, of langorousness and brilliance in scoring and expression that is overwhelming. At first Mahler composed settings for six translations of ancient Chinese songs, and then, discovering their musical affinity, bound them together into a symphonic conception by the introduction of two orchestral episodes. Realistic music at first sight—note the 'bird music' of the final movement, the illustrative use of mandoline, harp, and tambourine in the bright middle movements—*Das Lied von der Erde* establishes itself as a 'psychological' record of the composer's hopes and fears. Thus Mahler is in the line of descent from Schumann and Wolf (whom Mahler knew when he was a student).

Mahler, a Jew, was both proud and ambitious. Spurred on, as were many members of his race in Austria at the beginning of the century, he pursued his predestined course with inexorable determination. It was not easy. For in his early years he had incurred the hostility of Brahms. 'I shall', it is written in the last section of *Das Lied von der Erde*, 'no longer seek the far horizon.' As a composer Mahler was ever in search of the far horizon. Thus he invariably thought as a tone-poet and found it necessary to 'explain' his music by programmes. The second, third, and fourth symphonies (in which voices are employed and in which settings of poems from the romantic anthology *Das Knaben Wunderhorn* are introduced) centre on the personal quest for religious faith. And here it may be noted that Mahler became a convert to Roman

Catholicism, which fact led in 1906 to the composition of the most remarkable of the symphonies, the eighth. This, the 'symphony of a thousand', employing a vast orchestra, soloists, boys' choir, and double chorus, is built round the plainsong theme *Veni Creator Spiritus*, and the last scene from Goethe's *Faust*. For the performance of this mammoth symphony a special hall had to be built in Munich in 1910.

This, perhaps, is sufficient to show that in such music symphony had reached the limits of its expansion, and the composer the fullest inflation of his ego. It was time to put the clock back.

IX. On Performance and Interpretation

AIMING AT PERFECTION · The problem might be set in its simplest terms: the right notes in the wrong way, or the wrong notes in the right way? We may start at home. One's daughter may be preparing an examination piece, say a piano sonata by Mozart. Studiously attentive to all the instructions of her teacher she plays with great correctness. And yet one is grateful when her practice ends. For her presentation carries nothing of the quality, as we have learned to recognize it, of Mozart. Yet, impatient of the set task, she may turn the pages of her book and essay a sight reading of something unfamiliar. Wrong notes all over the place; but it sounds, nonetheless, like, say, Handel. In some way—not unconnected with the reassertion of her own natural vivacity—she has brought something to life. That is the crucial word.

Any musical performance must have vitality, and this must be instantly recognizable. At first sight this might appear to present no great difficulty to the skilled performer, or conductor. It is, however, alarming to note how many performers, complacently competent, are lacking in this respect. On the other hand there is sometimes too much display of the spurious vitality which virtuosity tends to incubate. For instance: speed presents one set of hazards, and expression another; so that Mozart is more often than not run off his feet, and Beethoven subjected to refinements more proper to Mendelssohn. The impression given by some conductors is that the music of the ancients being—as near as makes no odds—dead requires artificial respiration. This by the unwary is confused with inspiration.

On the other hand there are those whose absorption in the now fashionable province of musicology is such that anything 'un-authentic' is anathema. The frequent result is the production of all the right notes in the right *tempi* by the right, if often archaic, instruments; but without imagination. Dogma is not the best of aids to artistic perception; a point which the amateur, who swears the infallibility of one artist against the fallibility of another, might also recognize.

There is an essay somewhere by Charles Lamb in which he refers to the necessity for 'losing himself in other men's minds'. There is the key to musical interpretation, and to its understanding. Obviously it has some connection with 'life', as above.

A perfect interpretation of a musical work being as impossible of attainment as, according to Louis MacNeice, is a perfect translation of a poem, we should address ourselves to the situation in which we now are—in which gramophone record reviews, especially, are inclined to see perfection when it does not exist. It is pertinent to see what changes have taken place so that we can appreciate the growth of current fashions.

❲ PHILHARMONIC CONCERT 1828 · It is a hundred and thirty years since the Philharmonic Society gave a performance of Beethoven's *Pastoral Symphony*, of which this was the account. 'The Pastoral Symphony, both as a musical composition and descriptive piece, grows in esteem by frequent hearing; it only wants abridgement, particularly in the *andante*, to make it welcome to all lovers of grand orchestral performances. In its present state, with a slow movement, a quarter of an hour long, it is difficult, if not impossible, to find even a confirmed *fanatico* who does not think, whatever he may confess, that it hangs heavy.' (This is a reminder of a similar sentiment evoked from some by contemporary performances of symphonies by Mahler.) There can be read into that account the interpretation (or rather lack of interpretation) by Mr Neate who then occasionally conducted the Philharmonic Society's concerts.

The general listener, as opposed to the specialist student, is not aware in the *andante* of the *Pastoral Symphony* that there are twelve quavers in the bar. All he knows is that the music moves on and on. The brook: isn't that what the music is about? But become aware of the twelve quavers per bar through such clumsiness (which he mistook for 'correctness') as Mr Neate's and the fancy is shattered. Mr Neate's audience was moving away from the mundane—but not too far.

At the same Philharmonic concert a new work was performed: a concertante for aeol-harmonium and two guitars. The very combination for some enterprising contemporary of ours. But in 1828 'much disapprobation was expressed at the introduction of this, which was considered more fit for an exhibition-room than for a concert of so high an order. At the conclusion some hissing was heard, and many voices exclaimed, "Shame; Shame!" which, we fear, the very ingenious performers took to themselves, though meant to be addressed only to those who invited them there.' Fun and games were out. Music in 1828 must be invested with some degree of high seriousness.

⁋ GERMAN 'CORRECTNESS' · A critic who now summarizes a performance as 'adequate' may be taken as intending no compliment. Yet until well on into the nineteenth century adequacy was accepted as excellence. Knowing Mendelssohn's music it is difficult to associate its lightness and delicacy with the elegant, but *kapellmeister* character of his orchestral conducting. And when lesser luminaries directed operations the resulting interpretations were quite intolerable.

So at Munich once, when Mozart's G minor symphony (K.550) was in the programme we read how for Richard Wagner 'the lightly floating *andante* was converted into a ponderous *largo*; not the hundredth part of the weight of a single quaver was spared us; stiff and ghostly, like a bronze pigtail, the *battuta* of the *andante* was swung over our heads; even the feathers of the angels' wings

were turned into corkscrew curls—rigid; like those of the Seven
Years' War. Already I felt myself placed under the staff of a
Prussian recruiting officer.'

Now, we should be on Wagner's side. Clearly he was right.
But the Munich *kapellmeister* was obeying a tradition. That was
how he had been brought up to play Mozart, and his audiences—
with the exception of Wagner—thought it not improper. Nor
did they probably miss as much as we might think they did. For
they learned how to recreate for themselves. The fact that domes-
tic music-making was so widely practised, that the classics were
known through piano duet arrangements, suggest that the nineteenth century concert-goer was often further advanced in musical
perception than his modern counterpart—who looks for more
spoon-feeding.

In the companion book on *Concerto* it is explained how notes
on a printed score can come to life in the imagination. Similarly
the sounds indifferently produced may yet stimulate a vigorous
imaginative response, given the necessary effort. J. C. Bach, Abel,
Dittersdorf occur in the programmes of amateur societies, of
school orchestras. Imperfect performances no doubt; but often
surprisingly effective introductions to the more charming corners
of the eighteenth-century repertoire. Sincerity on the one side
and good will on the other count for a great deal in musical
understanding.

¶ THE 'ART' OF CONDUCTING · It is not surprising that a hundred years ago the norm was correctness. For the conductor
there was an innovation; Haydn, we may remember, in old age
still directed his symphonies from the keyboard, even though it
was no longer necessary to 'fill in' the harmonies. Nor is it surprising that the importance of the conductor's function should
increase as music became more complex in respect of colour and
rhythm. So Wagner's observations—in his essay *Über das Dirigen*
(*On Conducting*)—was timely. If he had not made them someone
else would.

In Germany, he said, orchestras had not increased their string
strength to balance the larger complement of wind. The numbers
of string players quoted on p. 27 would have been unthinkable

before Wagner. Now, of course, there are in 'symphony orches-
tras' rather too many string players for classical works. (Some
conductors do reduce their strength to produce a better balance.)
Wagner suggested that orchestras needed to rehearse adequately.
In this connection he drew attention to the good example of
Habeneck—founder of the *Société des Concerts du Conservatoire* in
Paris, and the first to introduce Beethoven's symphonies to
France—who rehearsed the *Choral Symphony* for three whole days,
until the players had completely absorbed the spirit of the com-
poser. Such devotion, alas! is not yet an economic possibility.

Orchestral music, Wagner went on, should sing. (Where he
used 'sing' we now use 'phrase', as the basis of fluency.) The conductor should adjust his ideas on *tempo* until he found that which
gave the music the opportunity to sing. So he distinguished between Beethoven, whose *adagios* could hardly be taken too slowly
and Mozart, whose *allegros* could hardly be taken too fast. The
long-term effect of Wagner's preaching may be realized from
Bruno Walter's recorded rehearsal of Mozart's 'Linz' symphony
in which the interpretation is essentially a 'singing' interpretation.

And then there was the value of *rubato*, that most difficult
quality effectively to apply. Yet without it music, even classical
music, would appear to us as mechanical, lifeless. Handel and
Bach, Mozart and Haydn—did they indulge in *rubato*? Probably
not—but interpretation requires always that music should seem
to be brought to life by the particular audience. So it is that the
'spirit of the age' will, often unconsciously, infect works of
another age. The judicious conductor, the experienced listener,
will know where the dividing line is between making the composer's intentions explicit and replacing them by arbitrary in-
dulgences of the self-centred.

❡ MODERN EMINENCES · Through Wagner came a new school
of conductors—von Bülow, Richter, Levi; Nikisch, Mottl, Wein-
gartner. In them was the conductor-cult born. They, gradually
displacing singers and pianists, became the Great Chams of music.
It was not for nothing that Richter—whose long years in England
exerted a strong influence—was known to his friends as 'the
king'. Gradually the quality of music itself became subordinate to

the great man's 'interpretation'. Toscanini's Beethoven, Klemperer's Beethoven, Boult's Beethoven. All very stimulating, but what matters is Beethoven's Beethoven, of which we may often be aware—but not always.

It is tempting to keep one's ears, or eyes (for the virtuoso conductor consciously sets out to be an eyeful) on irrelevancies. So long has this been going on that it has now become normal. Fifty years ago Charles Graves pointed out the dangers of misapplied enthusiasm. His words are apt.

'Instrumentalists and conductors', he wrote in *The Spectator* in 1908, 'have come to their own, and the *Prima donna* and the pianist no longer enjoy a monopoly of adulation. But while the modern cult of the orchestra from the point of view of the audience makes in the main for a deeper and more intelligent appreciation of the music that counts, it is not so easy to express unreserved satisfaction with the results in so far as they affect composers and conductors. The greater the number of people who enjoy the technique of orchestration, the greater is the inducement to composers to lavish their energies on non-essentials. Not long ago an English statesman observed that any fool could annex. Varying that formula, it is hardly too much to say that nowadays almost any clever pupil can score for a full orchestra. A lack of ideas matters little if you can show off the band, pile up sonorous climaxes, exploit the eccentric tones and extreme registers of special instruments, and, above all, create an atmosphere. What a writer . . . said . . . of Debussy—that his music is "all adjectives, and it is left to the interpreter to supply the noun"— can certainly be predicated with a considerable truth of a good deal of modern impressionist music.'

❡ NOUNS AND ADJECTIVES · As has been shown in earlier pages of this book composition itself has, in large part, got rid of adjectives. Hence the 'austerity' of Bartók, Stravinsky, Schoenberg, and those affected by their example. But the audience, one feels, accustomed to other garish influences, still looks for adjectival qualification. Music in performance must be 'robust', 'warm', 'pellucid', 'entreating', string tone must be 'silky', the brass 'resonant', the woodwind 'succulent',

'What', says a friend, 'do these terms mean?' In the long run not very much. Different orchestras develop different traditions as was lately shown by the visits of the Boston Symphony Orchestra (fine in virtuoso music but straining at the leash in the classics) and the Dresden Orchestra (studious and with ample middle-register tone). The great orchestras of the world are technically very proficient. How they play is a matter for the conductor. So we are brought back to him whose sole prerogative it is to 'interpret'.

'There are', wrote Martin Cooper, 'concert-goers who study the form of their favourite conductor or pianist with all the enthusiasm, if rather less than the expert knowledge, of the sporting enthusiast.'

An interesting occupation, but—*ce n'est pas la musique*. How, then, do we know a 'good' performance? Only, I think, by sensing that in a performance is enshrined the vision of the composer. And how do we know that? By listening to music of all sorts with an open mind, and by thinking on the music rather than the performance. That, I suspect, our great-grandfathers were better at than often we are.

INDEXES

Index of Works and Recordings

The following index gives publishers and selected long-playing recordings of the principal works mentioned in the text. Publishers are abbreviated thus (italic type denotes that a miniature score is available):

A, Augener
B & H, Boosey and Hawkes
Br., Breitkopf
C, Chester
E, Eulenberg
L, Lengnick

N, Novello
OUP, Oxford University Press
R, Ricordi
Si, Simrock
Sch, Schott
UE, Universal Edition

ABEL, Carl (1725–87), Symphony in E flat;[1] *R*;[2] Oiseau-Lyre OL 50118
ARNOLD, Malcolm (b. 1921),
   Symphony no. 2, Op. 40; *Patterson*; Philips NBL 5021

[1] Among Mozart's symphonies as K. 18.
[2] N.B. various symphonies by Abel, Arne, J. C. Bach, Dittersdorf, Filtz, Gossec, Gyrowetz, Holzbauer, and Stamitz are edited by A. Carse and published by Augener (score and parts).

BACH, John Christian (1735–82),
   3 symphonies, Op. 9; *E*;[1] Oiseau-Lyre OL 50007
   6 symphonies, Op. 18; *E*;[2] Philips ABR 4005

BALAKIREV, Mily (1837–1910), Symphony in C; Zimmerman; Columbia 33
   CX 1002

BARBER, Samuel (b. 1910), Symphony no. 2, Op. 19; *Schirmer*; Decca LX 3050

BAX, Arnold (1883–1953), Symphonies 1–6; *Murdoch*.

BEETHOVEN, Ludwig van (1770–1827), Symphonies:
     no. 1 in C, Op. 21; *B & H, E, R*; HMV ALP 1324
     no. 2 in D, Op. 36; *B & H, E, R*; HMV ALP 1145
     no. 3 in E flat ('Eroica'), Op. 55; *B & H, E, R*; Columbia 33 CX 1346
     no. 4 in B flat, Op. 60; *B & H, E, R*; Decca LXT 2847
     no. 5 in C mi., Op. 67; *B & H, E, R*; Columbia 33 CX 1077
     no. 6 in F ('Pastoral'), Op. 68; *B & H, E, R*; HMV ALP 1268
     no. 7 in A, Op. 92; *B & H, E, R*; Columbia 33 CX 1379
     no. 8 in F, Op. 93; *B & H, E, R*; Decca LXT 5232
     no. 9 in D mi. ('Choral'), Op. 125; *B & H, E, R*; HMV ALP 1286–7

BERLIOZ, Hector (1803–69),
   Symphonie fantastique, Op. 14; *E*; HMV ALP 1384

BIZET, Georges (1838–75), Symphony in C; *UE*; Decca LXT 5030

BORODIN, Alexander (1833–87), Symphonies:
     no. 1 in E flat; *B & H*; Columbia 33C X 1356
     no. 2 in B mi.; *B & H*; HMV CLP 1075
     no. 3 in A mi. (unfinished); *E*; HMV CLP 1075

BOYCE, William (1710–79),
   Symphonies 1–8 (ed. C. Lambert); OUP; Brunswick AXTL 1002–3

BRAHMS, Johannes (1833–97), Symphonies:
     no. 1 in C mi., Op. 68; *B & H*; Nixa NCL 16000
     no. 2 in D, Op. 73; *B & H*; Nixa 16001
     no. 3 in F, Op. 90; *B & H*; Nixa NCL 16002
     no. 4 in E mi., Op. 98; *B & H* ; Nixa NCL 16003
   Serenades:
     no. 1 in D, Op. 11; *E*; Brunswick AXTL 1026
     no. 2 in A, Op. 16; *E*.

BRITTEN, Benjamin (b. 1913),
   Sinfonia da Requiem; Op. 20; *B & H*; Decca LXT 2981

BRUCKNER, Anton (1824–96), Symphonies:
     no. 3 in D mi.; *E*; Decca LXT 2967
     no. 4 in E flat ('Romantic'); *E*; Columbia 33 CX 1274
     no. 5 in B flat; *E*; Decca LXT 5255–6
     no. 6 in A; *E*; Nixa WLP 6201

       [1] No. 2 in E flat.   [2] No. 4 in D.

---

[1] See f.n. 2 on p. 141.   [2] Eastman School of Music Publications.

K

HAYDN, Joseph (1732–1809), Symphonies:

    no. 54 in G; Br.; Nixa LLP 8032

    no. 60 in C ('Il distratto'); Br.; HMV ALP 1114

    no. 67 in F; Br.; Philips ABL 3075

    no. 80 in D mi.; Br.; Nixa WLP 5050

    no. 83 in G ('La poule'); *E*; HMV ALP 1038

    no. 84 in E flat; Br.; HMV CLP 1009

    no. 85 in B flat ('La reine'); *E*.

    no. 86 in D; *E*; HMV CLP 1009

    no. 88 in G; *E*; Decca LXT 5040

    no. 92 in G ('Oxford'); *E*; Columbia 33 CX 1028

    no. 93 in D; *E*; Columbia 33 CX 1038

    no. 94 in G ('Surprise'); *E*; Columbia 33 CX 1104

    no. 95 in C mi.; *E*; HMV ALP 1155

    no. 96 in D ('Miracle'); *E*; Philips ABL 3123

    no. 97 in C; *E*; Nixa WLP 5062

    no. 99 in E flat; *E*; Nixa WLP 5102

    no. 100 in G ('Military'); *E*; Decca LXT 2984

    no. 101 in D ('Clock'); *E*; Decca LXT 5040

    no. 102 in B flat; *E*; Decca LXT 2984

    no. 103 in E flat ('Drum roll'); *E*; Columbia 33 CX 1104

    no. 104 in D ('London'); *E*; HMV CLP 1055

HEILLER, Anton (b. 1923) *Kammersymphonie*; UE

HONEGGER, Arthur (b. 1892), *Skating-Rink*, *Tanz Symphonie*; UE

KABALEVSKY, Dimitri (b. 1904),

    Symphony no. 2 in C mi, Op. 19; B & H[1]; Capitol CCL 7502

KŘENEK, Ernst (b. 1900),

    3 symphonies, Op. 7, 12, 16; UE

    Kleine symphonie, Op. 58; UE

MAHLER, Gustav (1860–1911), Symphonies:

    no. 1 in D; UE; Philips ABL 3044

    no. 2 in C mi.; UE; Vox PL 7012

    no. 4 in G; UE; Columbia 33 CX 1034

    no. 5 in C sharp mi.; *E*; Nixa WLP 6207

    no. 6 in A mi.; Bote & Boch; Philips ABL 3103–4

    no. 7 in E mi. ('Tragic'); Bote & Boch; Nixa WLP 6211

    no. 8 in E flat; UE; Philips ABL 3024–5

    no. 9 in D; UE; Columbia 33 CX 1250–1

    no. 10 in F sharp (unfinished); UE; Nixa WLP 6207

[1] For Anglo-Soviet Music Press Ltd.

---

[1] Complete set of symphonies in miniature score in 2 vols., pub. Ricordi.

I wish to acknowledge the assistance of Mr L. W. Duck, of the Henry Watson Music Library, in compiling this index.

General Index

Abel, Carl, 12, 20, 31, 81, 82–3, 136
Alfvén, Hugo, 33, 37
Altmann, Wilhelm, 111
Antheil, George, 37
Arne, T. A., 82
Arnold, Malcolm, 37, 40
Artaria, publisher, 97

Bach, Carl Philipp Emanuel, 12, 19, 81, 83
Bach, Johann Christoph Friedrich, 12, 83
Bach, Johann Sebastian, 13, 23, 25, 28, 34, 82, 84, 91, 94, 110, 115, 119, 137
Bach, John Christian, 12, 31, 81, 82–4, 85, 88, 136
Balakirev, Mily, 122, 123
Bantock, Granville, 57, 63
Barber, Samuel, 13, 40, 49
Barbirolli, John, 45
Bartók, Béla, 138
Bax, Arnold, 42, 57–8, 62
Beethoven, Ludwig van, 12, 13, 15, 22–3, 24, 28, 32, 35, 42, 55, 59, 65–80, 84, 98, 99, 100, 102, 103, 105, 110, 112, 113, 126, 128, 134, 137, 138
Bennett, W. Sterndale, 112

Berg, Alban, 42, 131
Berlioz, Hector, 23, 29, 32, 36, 69, 85, 107, 112, 117, 121, 123, 128, 130
Bizet, Georges, 117–18
Borodin, Alexander, 25, 122, 123–4
Böttger, Adolph, 110
Boult, Adrian, 138
Bourges, Michel, 85
Boyce, William, 81–2
Brahms, Johannes, 12, 24, 26, 29, 33, 35, 39, 43, 60, 63, 100, 111–16, 123, 126, 128, 131
Brian, Havergal, 57
Britten, Benjamin, 40, 50–1
Bruckner, Anton, 12, 24, 34, 36, 115, 127–30
Bülow, Hans von, 115, 137
Bush, Alan, 47

Carpani, Giuseppe, 95
Casella, Alfredo, 100
Cherubini, Luigi, 99
Chopin, Frederick, 70
Clementi, Muzio, 100
Coleridge, S. T., 53
Cooper, Martin, 139
Copland, Aaron, 13, 40, 49
Cowell, Henry, 49